TRADES & INDUSTRIES OF NORWICH

Joyce Gurney-Read

with a foreword by
John Taylor

G

Gliddon Books
Norwich, Norfolk

To Clare and Tony, Suzanne
and Paul

Published 1988

© Joyce Gurney-Read
© Foreword with John Taylor

Printed by Crowes of Norwich

ISBN 0 947893 09 1

Contents

Foreword

by

'BBC Radio Norfolk's John Taylor'

Times change and we — alas — change with them. To many of the people who pick up this book the firms and the personalities which Joyce Gurney-Read has made the subject of her painstaking researches will mean very little. Chamberlins! Caleys! Rumsey Wells! Just names — and to the teenager who walks along the newly emerging pavements of Gentleman's Walk as remote and unfamiliar as a cloche hat or a jar of hundreds and thousands.

But to my own generation, the thousands of people who grew up in Norwich and its surrounding area between the two world wars, these names take on a lasting significance. How could we forget them? They were part of our lives. As a small child I was wheeled in what was then called a perambulator past the wide windows of Chamberlins store. When, a little later, I first walked through the gates of Norwich School — this would be in 1932 — it was in a blazer supplied by Mr Rumsey Wells from his queer little shop in St Andrew's Street. When, a little later still, I shuffled into a public house and drank my first pint of beer it was a pint of Steward and Patterson's bitter — and it had some guts in it.

There are other names, of course, which it is impossible to forget: Caley's the chocolate factory (does anyone remember the famous 'Marching Chocolate'?), Bullards' brewery, the Boulton & Paul engineering works. Some of them still survive. Mrs Gurney-Read has examined them all and the results are chronicled in the succeeding pages. Her researches will be of great interest not simply to the people who worked for these companies, or those with some more remote connection, but to the infinitely larger number interested in our Norfolk past. In my contributions to BBC Radio Norfolk and in answering the letters and enquiries of listeners, I am frequently astonished by the depth of interest in this local heritage. It would be misleading and demeaning to call such interest 'nostalgic' for it represents a much more fundamental awareness of the people and the places that went before us and how they coloured and continue to colour our existence.

Consequently, I hope that those of you who never tasted Caley's Marching Chocolate or drank a pint of Bullards' mild will read this volume with as much enthusiasm as those of us who can never eat a bar of chocolate or drink a glass of beer without thinking of their inferiority to what went before. Such things make up the paraphernalia of our lives. We could no sooner forget them than our own names, or the narrow Norwich streets where we were born.

JOHN TAYLOR

Acknowledgements

For giving me their time, and information on the Companies, sincere thanks to:-

Richard Bond: Bonds (Norwich) Limited
Gerald H. Bullard: Bullard & Sons Limited
Roger B. Copeman: John Copeman & Sons
Malcolm H. Jarvis: Boulton & Paul Limited
Marie Lee: Mann Egerton & Company Limited
Peter Lloyd: Barnards Limited
Peter V. Pank: Panks Engineers
Bryan C. Read: R. J. Read Limited
David J. H. White: James Southall & Company Limited
Michael J. Youngs: J. Youngs & Son
The Alfred Munning's Art Museum, Dedham, Essex

To many others who have helped with information and/or photographs, including David Jones and John Renton, Bridewell Museum (Norfolk Museums Service), Ernest Nicol, Printing Department, Norwich School of Art, the staff at the Local Studies Library, Rowntree Mackintosh, Ted Lewis (Booker plc), William H. Francis, Kate Matthews, Eastern Counties Newspapers, Members of N.I.A.S. for helpful comments, and Chris Barringer, without whose help and encouragement this book would not have been written.

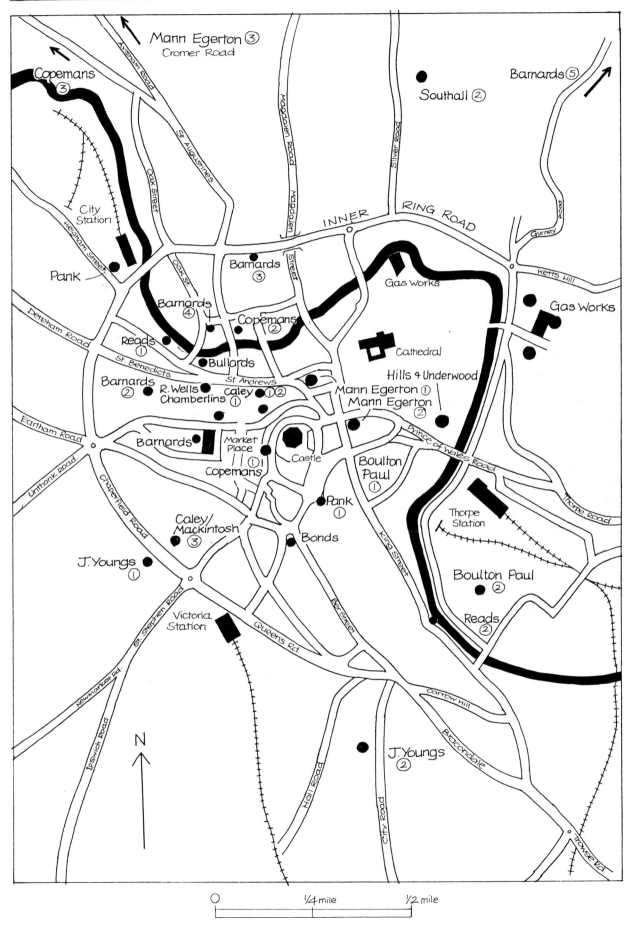

● Site. Numbers are those of sequence of sites eg. Youngs ① = First site Youngs ② etc.

Map by Ruth Murray

INTRODUCTION

"Have you visited Norwich before?" After asking that question a guide will almost certainly advise you to look at the Castle, the Cathedral and the Close, St. Peter Mancroft and the many other parish churches. To this list might be added the other city museums, the Sainsbury Centre of the University of East Anglia, the view of Norwich from St. James' Hill and so on. He or she may mention the Norwich Union with its logo of the Cathedral, Colmans because of mustard and then they will probably go on to suggest that the Broads, the bird enthusiasts' north coast, and the great rural churches and many fine houses should be visited.

It is doubtful if commercial and industrial Norwich would be mentioned in such an introduction. Yet despite the obvious attractions of such a tourist's guide Norwich has always been a busy commercial centre for what is perhaps the widest service area of any English county town. This in part stems from its having been the second city of England until the eighteenth century. Norfolk's main roads led to Norwich as did three of its railways; it is the spider in the middle of a web. Wool and later cloth, hemp and flax, wheat, malting barley, cattle, horses and sheep all poured in to the markets of the city and the merchants, lawyers, factors and dealers who organised this trade congregated in Norwich. These raw materials supplied its early industries leather making, textiles, malting, brewing and milling and the many secondary industries that sprang from those primary ones. From the textile industry came the capital that was accumulated to establish banking and insurance; out of the leather and tanning industries the shoe industry evolved and as agriculture became mechanised so the engineering firms began to specialise in providing all sorts of farm equipment and machinery.

The trades and industries of Norwich have not received enough attention and this valuable set of case studies does much to redress this deficiency and to make us realise just what a wealth of interest lies in the stories of growth, change or decline that they reveal.

Sir Robert Bignold's story of his own family and of their connection with the Norwich Union, and Terry Gourvish's recent study of Steward and Patteson are exceptions to this statement and several other studies have given background material to the story of Norwich industries. *Norwich in the Nineteenth Century* and Hawkins' social study of the city at the beginning of this century outline the beginnings of much of the present industry of the city as do *Norwich and its Region* and the *Norfolk We Live In*. *Norwich a Time of Opportunity* by Peter Townroe is the most up-to-date review of the state of the economy of the city. The broad trends and general statements in all these texts conceal a fascinating mixture of histories of success, experiment and decline.

Some of the firms that became household names such as Boulton and Paul have ceased manufacturing in Norwich. Perhaps it is most surprising of all that beer is no longer brewed in Norwich nor malt made there. Bullards, Steward and Patteson and Youngs Crawshay & Youngs were major employers in Norwich from the 1850's until the 1950's. They were carnivores of the smaller breweries both in Norwich and in the market towns of Norfolk and finally they themselves were eaten by the bigger animals in the interests of the 'economies of scale'. Norwich Bitter is now brewed in Manchester and London! Hills and Underwood was an interesting variant on brewing for vinegar instead of for beer. The shape of the malt-kiln, with its distinctive top has survived to become an accepted 'vernacular' element in later buildings: Norwich council housing in Conisford and new office blocks in Yarmouth carry echoes of the kiln's distinctive shape. The only survivors of the link with the cereal growing of the surrounding region are the flour mills in the city. Read's, with a once-used river side position, still draws grain from many miles outside Norwich and the queue of huge lorries beside the mill is a forceful reminder of the way the city still links up with the farms of the richest grain growing lands in England.

In terms of numbers of employees boot and shoe manufacture came top of the list of industries in Norwich after 1850. Great changes have taken place and quality of product has replaced sheer volume of production as a measure of success. Just as British supplies of hides gave way to those from the New World so competition from other mass producers hae reduced the number of British manufacturers.

The account of James Southall & Co shows how increasingly complex machinery has reduced the labour force in the shoe industry but allowed it to specialise and survive with its famous Start-Rite range. As with the textile industry city and county were often linked by outreach work in the shoe industry.

In later volumes other raw material based firms will be considered — Colmans being an obvious example. All the firms using raw materials from the surrounding farmlands triggered off a wealth of supporting industries especially the metal using industries that began to serve fast-changing agriculture with its fencing, its machinery and its specialised buildings. Joyce Gurney-Read's description of Boulton and Paul in 1869 emphasises that W. S. Boulton was a manufacturer of agricultural and horticultural implements. Earlier still as she points out Charles Barnard, a farmer's son, realised the importance of fencing to keep out rabbits and by 1844 he was 'weaving' wire fencing.

Caleys (Rowntree Mackintosh) are not easy to categorise. We do not know why A. J. Caley, a chemist, came to Norwich. He discovered a new market — that for a wide range of mineral waters — which may in part have stemmed from the poor quality of the city's drinking water as outlined by John Pound in *Norwich in the Nineteenth Century*. His imaginative leap into chocolate parallels that of Walls into ice-cream. He had a factory and workers, and the reverse of Walls, he looked for cold season products. Caley brought in the Swiss methods of chocolate making — an interesting point in view of the final purchase of Caley's descendants by Nestlés! Chamberlins, like Bonds, became a Norwich retailing institution and the contemporary account of a store that set out to serve the county as well as the city gives a fascinating glimpse of an era now gone. Rumsey Wells must have added considerable life and amusement to St. Andrews Street: it is not clear as to what the pre-Wells use of the Cockey Lane premises was. Perhaps, like Chamberlins, they can be viewed as being descendants of the former important textile industry and the clothing industry that grew out of it.

It is possible to see broad explanations as to why certain groups of industrial or commercial activity developed in Norwich but frequently it is an individual or a pair of individuals with complementary skills that sets up a new or exceptionally dynamic business. Boulton and Paul, Mann and Egerton are good examples described in this book and Laurence Scott is another. Many of the leading figures in Norwich firms became Sheriffs, Lord Mayors and/or benefactors of the city. Bullards is perhaps the outstanding example of such a firm examined in this book.

The two World Wars have had a great effect on many of the businesses described. Boulton & Paul's contribution to aircraft and later to airship manufacture is well known and was noted in Walter Kershaw's mural shown on the cover but that of Mann Egerton as an aircraft maker is less well known. Barnards produced miles of netting for desert roads in World War I and vast quantities of shells, amongst other things, in the Second World War. Caley's benefited in the First War with demands for their Marching Chocolate. Copeman, Chamberlins and Rumsey Wells all received major fillips to their businesses as a result of wartime commissions. War damage led to a great increase in work for Youngs as they rebuilt Mackintosh's and Bonds. Boulton & Paul's strategically important site was hit several times in the Second World War air raids. Ironically it seems that most Norwich firms received additional demands for their products as a result of the two great war efforts.

A characteristic of late twentieth century industry is its national and multi-national nature: fewer and fewer firms have a purely Norwich base. Bonds is now a part of the John Lewis partnership, the businesses have gone national and are only part of huge conglomerates; the intimate link between business and its 'home' city is fast disappearing.

These then are some of the categories and characteristics of the manufacturing and trading firms of Norwich during the late nineteenth and the first threequarters of the twentieth century. The case studies that follow and that have been carefully researched by Joyce Gurney-Read, often with much help from the businesses described, provide us with a new look at one aspect of Norwich that has been too little studied.

Christopher Barringer

JAMES SOUTHALL & CO. LTD.

It appears from city records that leather and shoemaking played an important part in the life of the city from as early as the 13th century. There are frequent references to parmenters (leather workers) and cordwainers (shoemakers). The name of one of our churches in King Street, St. Peter Parmentergate, and streets formerly called Saddlegate and Cordwainers' Row, bear testimony to their importance.

Shoes were an important mark of social class. The labouring classes would have made their own, whilst master shoe-makers, employing apprentices, fashioned footwear for the landowners and gentry of the neighbourhood.

Charles Winter – Lord Mayor of Norwich in 1851.
One time owner of Southalls.

James Southall & Company can trace their origins to the latter part of the 18th century, when, James Smith a leather seller and shoemaker, with a shop on Norwich Market Place started making ready-made shoes. Charles Winter, James Smith's grandson, took over the business in 1816, and introduced machines from America for sewing uppers. Subsequently he bought machines for stitching soles to uppers at the rate of a pair per minute. In this way a pair of boots could be cut out, and the uppers, after fitting, sewn together and finished in an hour; and the work, moreover, was more skilfully completed. Three operatives were required for each machine, two fitters and one machinist.

Sales increased, both for the home and colonial market. By 1860 Thomas, Singer and Howes hand machines were in use in the factory at Nos. 7, 8 and 9 Upper Market, and later steam power was introduced to work the machinery.

Mr. Winter, who lived in Heigham Grove, was, in the manner of most Victorian businessmen, prominent in social, civic and political life. Sheriff in 1846, he became a magistrate, and was elected Mayor of Norwich in 1851. There is a monument to his memory in St. Peter Mancroft church. After his death the business was taken over by John Willis and James Southall. They maintained the reputation of the company, improved the quality of the merchandise, and carried on a large export trade to Canada, the Cape of Good Hope and India. After Willis died the business was carried on by James Southall and his two sons Charles and Frederick, and became a Limited Company.

In 1891 Bernard James Hanly joined the company as Manufacturing Manager. Born in 1872 at Colchester and educated at Trinity House School, he had been on the staff of S.A. Morgan & Co., shoe manufacturers, before joining Southall.

The original factory in the parish of St. Peter Mancroft is now only a memory. In 1904 it was described as having a leather warehouse, counting house, warehouse for 'bottom stuff', and an additional storehouse where thousands of pairs of

1

JAMES SOUTHALL & CO. LTD.

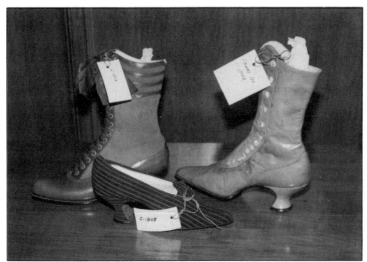

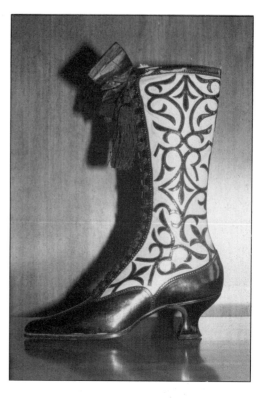

Early fashion shoes and boots displayed in the firm's boardroom.

higher grade ladies' and children's boots and shoes, and men's light and fancy footwear were stored. The sample room is said to have contained specimens of high-grade footwear, brocaded and plain evening shoes, hand-made goods and children's shoes and sandals. There were 20 different sorts of machines, operated by girls and women.

Technical innovation continued to improve the firm's efficiency. The Amazeen Skiving Machine, for instance, did in an hour what it took a day to do by hand, also the machine was more precise: One straight sewing machine made 3,000 stitches a minute. Other machines were the Lufkin Folding Machine, Wheel & Wilson's Closing Machine, Singer's Binder, and Singer's New Rapid Machine.

In the Turn-round Sewing Department, a transition in the trade could be seen. Almost all the men stood to do their work, but two or three of the old school found it impossible to accommodate themselves to the new order, and were seated. They would not have made a living wage if they had stood at their work, the younger men would have found it hard to sit and retain their efficiency.

Finishing and rubbing down the heels caused clouds of small particles of leather and dust. The machines were fitted with large fans, and pipes through which the dirt and dust were extracted and deposited as refuse outside the building. Possibly this may have been for the benefit of the workers, (there was not a Health & Safety at Work Act in those days!) but the dust could have caused serious problems if lodged in the machinery, to the detriment of the quality of the shoes.

Expansion continued and in 1907 a large new factory was erected on Crome Road, once part of the great Mousehold Heath, and overlooking the city. It was a one storey building, except for the Stock Room, and covered 62,000 square feet. The old factory remained in use until 1935 but was later swept away to clear the site for the new City Hall. In a 1910/11 Trade Directory James Southall & Co. Ltd., of Crome Road are offering specialities in fine footwear, 'The Lightfoot', 'The Sandringham Flexible' and 'The Satisfaction Welted'. They received the Diploma of Honour at the Franco-British Exhibition in 1908, the Diploma of Honour at the Bruxelles Exhibition in 1910, and the Grand Prix at Turin in 1911. Bernard Hanly married James Southall's youngest daughter, Mabel Rosa, in 1901. That same year he was appointed Managing Director, whilst Frederick Southall became Chairman. It was Bernard Hanly who piloted the firm through the trade depression of the 1920s and 1930s. He became Chairman and Managing Director in 1927, Sheriff and a magistrate in 1932, a Liberal Councillor from 1933 to 1936, and Chairman of the Company in 1937. He had two sons and two daughters.

In 1935 the firm was advertising *'The artistic traditions of the city and generations of skilled hand labour have made an indelible impression on the footwear produced, and which are in great demand, not only for the Home Market, but in every quarter of the globe. The prominent features of the output are the Start-rite brand of shoes for children, and Lightfoot and Jasco fashion and comfort shoes for ladies. Nearly 1,000 men and women are constantly employed and contribute largely to the prosperity of this renowned city.'* Prior to the Second World War their output was 11,500 pairs per week with a labour force of 850 people.

Bernard Hanly and Frederick Southall both died

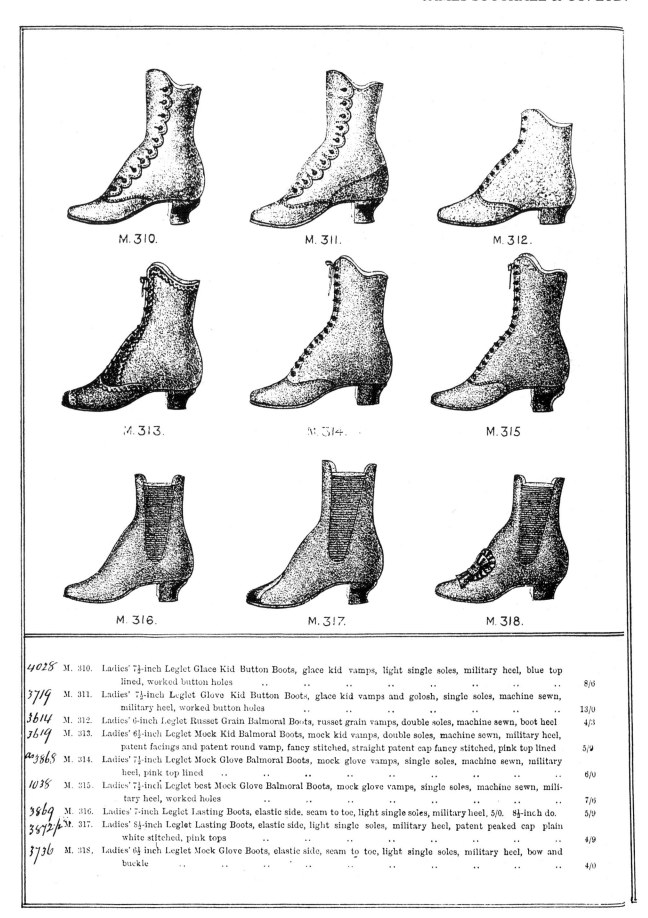

M. 310.   M. 311.   M. 312.

M. 313.   M. 314.   M. 315

M. 316.   M. 317.   M. 318.

4028	M. 310.	Ladies' 7½-inch Leglet Glace Kid Button Boots, glace kid vamps, light single soles, military heel, blue top lined, worked button holes	8/6
3719	M. 311.	Ladies' 7½-inch Leglet Glove Kid Button Boots, glace kid vamps and golosh, single soles, machine sewn, military heel, worked button holes	13/0
3614	M. 312.	Ladies' 6-inch Leglet Russet Grain Balmoral Boots, russet grain vamps, double soles, machine sewn, boot heel	4/3
3619	M. 313.	Ladies' 6½-inch Leglet Mock Kid Balmoral Boots, mock kid vamps, double soles, machine sewn, military heel, patent facings and patent round vamp, fancy stitched, straight patent cap fancy stitched, pink top lined	5/9
As 3868	M. 314.	Ladies' 7½-inch Leglet Mock Glove Balmoral Boots, mock glove vamps, single soles, machine sewn, military heel, pink top lined	6/0
1038	M. 315.	Ladies' 7½-inch Leglet best Mock Glove Balmoral Boots, mock glove vamps, single soles, machine sewn, military heel, worked holes	7/6
3869	M. 316.	Ladies' 7-inch Leglet Lasting Boots, elastic side, seam to toe, light single soles, military heel, 5/0. 8½-inch do.	5/9
3872/b	M. 317.	Ladies' 8½-inch Leglet Lasting Boots, elastic side, light single soles, military heel, patent peaked cap plain white stitched, pink tops	4/9
3736	M. 318.	Ladies' 6½-inch Leglet Mock Glove Boots, elastic side, seam to toe, light single soles, military heel, bow and buckle	4/0

JAMES SOUTHALL & CO. LTD.

LADIES' CASHMERE BOOTS.

SEW ROUNDS.

No.		Per Pair.
240	Black English Cashmere Boots, elastic sides, enamelled horse caps ..	2/0
241	Black English Cashmere Boots, side lace, enamelled horse caps ..	1/9
1	Black English Cashmere Boots, elastic sides, enamelled horse caps ..	2/4
2	Black English Cashmere Boots, side lace, enamelled horse caps ..	2/0
3	Black English Cashmere Boots, elastic sides, patent vamps ..	2/8
4	Black English Cashmere Boots, top pieces, elastic sides, patent vamps ..	2/11
5	Black English Cashmere Boots, elastic sides, patent caps ..	3/1
6	Black French Cashmere Boots, elastic sides, patent vamps ..	3/10
7	Black English Cashmere Boots, pumps, elastic sides, enamelled horse vamps ..	3/2
8	Black English Cashmere Boots, pumps, side lace, enamelled horse vamps ..	2/8

PUMPS.

9	Black English Cashmere Boots, side lace, enamelled horse vamps ..	3/2
11	Black English Cashmere Boots, elastic sides, enamelled horse vamps	3/9
10	Black French Cashmere Boots, military heels, elastic sides, patent calf caps ..	4/3
12	Black French Cashmere Boots, elastic sides, enamelled horse vamps ..	4/4
13	Black French Cashmere Boots, military heels, elastic sides, enamelled horse vps.	5/0
14	Black French Cashmere Boots, elastic sides, patent vamps ..	5/0
15	Black French Cashmere Boots, military heels, elastic sides, patent vamps ..	5/7
16	Black French Cashmere Boots, elastic sides, patent vamps ..	5/8
17	Black French Cashmere Boots, military heels, elastic sides, patent caps ..	7/9
18	Black French Cashmere Boots, military heels, elastic sides, patent caps ..	6/3
19	Black French Cashmere Boots, elastic sides, patent vamps ..	6/9

WELTS.

20	Black English Cashmere Boots, spring heels, side lace, patent vamps ..	3/1
21	Black English Cashmere Boots, spring heels, patent caps ..	4/0
22	Black English Cashmere Boots, spring heels, side lace, patent vamps ..	4/0
24	Black French Cashmere Boots, spring heels, side lace, patent vamps ..	4/7
27	Black French Cashmere Boots, extra lifts, elastic sides, patent vamps ..	6/6
28	Black French Cashmere Boots, extra lifts, elastic sides, patent vamps ..	7/0

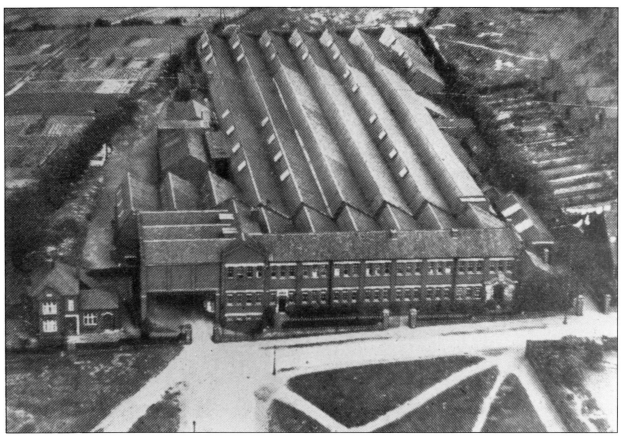

Aerial view of the factory in Crome Road, Norwich, in 1935.

on the same day in 1942, and Mr. James Laffan Hanly, Bernard's eldest son became Chairman.

The shoe trade was very labour intensive, but despite losing many operatives during the war years, they continued to cater for ladies and children. After hostilities ceased the firm started concentrating on the manufacture of children's shoes. The original Start-rite shoe was an adaptation of a patented design known as the 'Thomas heel', the chief characteristic being a V-shaped heel. A two-year nation-wide survey was carried out on children's feet in order to produce better fitting shoes, and from this evolved the unique foot measuring system used today, which ensures a comfortable and perfectly formed shoe to fit any size or shape of child's foot.

The famous Start-rite twins are now known all over the world. Recently posters have been used by Police forces around the country in their 'Say No to Strangers' campaign. Over 4,000 of the classic poster of the twins, overprinted with a warning to children not to talk to strangers, have been ordered, and used by officers to illustrate their talks to school-children.

Mr. James Hanly died in November, 1985, but the family tradition is being maintained, the present Chairman and Managing Director being his nephew, Mr. David White. The firm now employs approximately 700 employees at its various sites, selling one and a half million pairs of shoes annually

Poster by Sir Alfred Munnings

JAMES SOUTHALL & CO. LTD.

to over 1,200 stockists, and exporting to many
countries including Australasia, North America,
France and Southern Ireland.

CHILDREN'S SHOES HAVE FAR TO GO!

START-RITE

– AND THEY'LL WALK HAPPILY EVER AFTER

1951

JAMES SOUTHALL & CO. LTD., CROME ROAD, NORWICH

E
V
E
R
Y

D
E
P
A
R
T
M
E
N
T

B
U
I
L
T

A
N
D

S
U
S
T
A
I
N
E
D

B
Y

"
E
X
C
E
L
L
E
N
C
E
."

CHAMBERLINS LIMITED

Chamberlins' origins lie north of the border, in the person of a Scot, Henry Chamberlin (1777-1848) who came to Norwich from Edinburgh in 1814, and founded a department store on the corner of Dove Street and Guildhall Hill a year later. His son Robert joined him as a partner in 1823, the firm becoming known as Chamberlin Sons & Company – and it was he who was responsible for the development in the company's growth. He entered local politics in 1848, becoming Sheriff the same year, an Alderman in 1870 and Mayor in 1854, 1856 and 1871. Robert had seventeen children by two marriages, and two of his sons, Alexander (b.1835), and George (b.1846) were to play an important part in the history of the firm.

An intriguing description of the store comes from an article written at the turn of the century. *'The premises, which have been considerably enlarged and entirely re-arranged form a conspicuously handsome block. The main building is of red brick, faced with stone, and is of four stories in height, while the subsidiary portion, which extends nearly the whole length of Dove Street, is of three stories, the ground floor portion of this being entirely of glass. Five very spacious and handsome shop windows face the Market Place, or the corner, and there are two very fine entrances. The premises cover an area of 42,057 feet, and for elegance, comfort or completeness, they stand unrivalled by any similar establishment in the country.*

The stock kept on hand is of considerable value, goods to the amount of no less than £80,000 being available for customers to select from. The main shop is of considerable extent, and is, like all the other portions of this vast emporium, most elegantly fitted up, handsome glass cases serving to display articles of millinery, etc., of the richest description. This fine shop is warmed throughout with hot air, and is lighted by chandeliers of artistic design and elegant appearance. Handsome Corinthian pillars are located at intervals, and serve not only to support the superstructure, but to impart an imposing appearance to the fine vista presented by this richly decorated portion of the building.

Close to the main entrance is the millinery department – a richly decorated saloon, having a ceiling finely panelled and ornamented, four sculptured bosses marking the intersections of the beams in every instance. This section is lavishly provided with mirrors, and glass cases also give an elegant air to the room. Flowers are here tastefully arranged in cachepots, and the lighting is effected by chandeliers of exceptionally fine design. The buyer for this section, and also the head milliner, each visit Paris and London periodically, bringing back the latest and most fashionable models which are reproduced in the workrooms of this firm.

The mantle saloon also has a ceiling of rich design and fine execution. Cheval glasses are placed at frequent intervals, and mirrors are also

lavishly used as screens. Glass cases of artistic shape are used to display and protect examples of work, as are also tables formed of plate glass cases, which serve as tables, at the same time containing fur boas, ties, capes, muffs, etc., of great value.

The section appropriated to ladies' underclothing is also a rich saloon, divided into two parts by a richly worked open screen of wood. Adjoining the fitting rooms, from which it is divided by a screen of ornamental glass, is the fine waiting and writing room, which forms one of the most distinctive features of this splendid house. It is lighted with a central chandelier of artistic workmanship, having five shaded lights. This elegant room is well supplied with settees and lounges richly upholstered, and has escritoires and all the requisites for letter writing or correspondence. The tables are of handsome design, and are well supplied with magazines, newspapers, etc., and opening out from this room is a suite of retiring rooms, lavatories, etc. This novel department has been provided expressly for the country customers

of the house, and the ladies are much pleased with it. There is a Post Office box fixed at the chief entrance. The carpet and furnishing department is a well-appointed section, and is on the same level as the main shop. It is lighted by a well lantern, and is provided with pendants, having each two shaded burners. The gallery overhead is supported by fluted pillars of light construction. In the workshops carpets are made up by machinery, free of charge, and there is also a complete staff of upholsterers and others employed in the making up or fitting of bed furniture, hangings, or draperies, of every kind.

The dress department is considered by the principals as the chief one, and great attention is bestowed on it. It is a handsome square gallery, the centre of which is occupied by the lantern opening, which lights the department below. It has a glass roof and contains a very considerable counter space, while the walls are literally lined with shelves, containing all the best available fabrics of English or Continental make. A staff of one hundred and twenty skilled workwomen are employed in the

A corner of one of the retail showrooms.

work-rooms in connection with this important section, and even with this great staff the resources of the house are often severely taxed to execute the large number of orders with which the firm are favoured.

Another special feature of this superb establishment is the refreshment room, which is a spacious room fitted up and furnished in the most luxurious manner, and in the best possible taste. It has a buffet, well supplied by the articles in request by ladies, and the proprietors disclaim any intention of making a profit on the refreshments here supplied, the department having been provided for the convenience of the country customers, many of whom come long distances, and who fully appreciate the consideration shown for their comfort.'

When War broke out in August, 1914, the company's factory, by then situated in Botolph Street, was entirely devoted to the manufacture of civilian goods for the home and foreign markets. Almost immediately the call came for help, and so prompt was the response that within a month the business was almost entirely transferred to war productions. The difficulties, although enormous, were tackled so successfully that in a very short time the eight hundred employees were working at the highest pressure in order to satisfy Admiralty and War Office requests for an ever-increasing output.

For some years the company had been the sole concessionaires for Great Britain and the Colonies for the manufacture of Pegamoid waterproof clothing. In pre-war days the authorities had subjected this material to a severe test in all climates, and it was held in such high esteem that, with the exception of a certain quantity which went to the military and to the Italian Government, the Admiralty claimed the bulk of the Company's output during the whole period of the war.

Another important aspect of the Company's activities was the manufacture of East Coast oilskin water-proof material, and throughout the war this was used in many styles of garments for the sea and land forces. The demand became so pressing that not only was the entire output requisitioned by the Admiralty and War Office, but it was found necessary to build and equip a new factory in order to cope with it. In addition to these services the Company contracted for the supply of clothing to meet the requirements of the G.P.O., Government munition factories, and other important departments. At the request of the Government large quantities of standard clothes were also made, as well as suits for discharged soldiers. The war work of Chamberlins totalled close on one million garments, and they received from the authorities official recognition of the value of their services to the State in the years of the nation's peril. One hundred and twenty-five members of their Norwich staff enlisted and eight died in the service of their country. Many others served with distinction and obtained commissions and decorations for gallantry.

In 1935 the post-war years brought fresh demands

Chamberlin's removal van, 1911.

and challenges and, although maintaining old traditions, Chamberlins had moved with the times and presented modernized premises fully equipped to give service in all departments of drapery and house furnishing. Their factory, equipped with modern machinery, produced speciality men's sports clothing under their registered brand 'Sartella'. They remained a large manufacturer of oilskins whose largest customer was the British Government.

It was a pleasure to shop at Chamberlins in the 'thirties' and 'forties'. You were welcomed by a floor walker, who escorted you to the desired department. The little drawers under and behind the counters were filled with an amazing array of items

for sale, all of which were displayed with great artistry on the counter for the customer's perusal. Chairs were provided for all to sit upon, and the goods selected were duly packed, and would be delivered to your home if required. The lady assistants, who were apprenticed and often lived over the shop, were not allowed to serve customers for the first year, but fetched and carried for their superiors. Later they would be allowed to assist the seniors, and it was only during their third year they were allowed to deal directly with the customers.

Such old world charm could not resist the march of time. This lovely, elegant store was taken over by Marshall & Snelgroves in the 1950s and nothing now remains to remind us of Chamberlins of Norwich.

Chamberlins Ltd, 1935.

J. YOUNGS & SON – BUILDERS

Youngs were another firm with a mid-19th century foundation. The founder, James Youngs came from Alburgh and is thought to have been engaged as a bricklayer building railway bridges for the Eastern Counties Railway, getting nearer and nearer to Norwich as the rail network expanded. Three years after his arrival in Norwich he set up on his own account as a carpenter and joiner, in Chapel Field Road, and in 1851 laid the foundations of a large and extensive firm.

As the city expanded in the 1850s this was the great age of speculative building. During the first few years he built over 1,000 houses in this way, some of which were in Heigham Street, West Wymer Street and Trory Street. Subsequently he was rewarded by consistent commercial success. The Youngs' works faced Chapel Field Road, bounded on one side by Essex Street, and on the other side by Bristol Terrace. The premises were expanded to include timber sheds, mason's shop, machine room and paint stores, together with plumbers', carpenters' and joiners' shops, and an ironmongery store. Glass was securely packed in large cases in a warehouse adjoining the paint store, and nearby were additional sheds for the storage and seasoning of large quantities of walnut, oak, mahogany, pitchpine and other woods. Cement stores and nail house were in separate departments, the latter containing tons of nails. Stables adjoined the workshops and the store yard behind the United Methodist Free Church was full of timber, scaffolding and other builders' materials.

In 1870 James was joined by his son John, born 10th October, 1855, and educated at Gurney House School, Magdalen Street. Sixteen years later he became a full partner. (John Youngs was Councillor for Nelson Ward for many years. He died in 1929).

Gradually, domestic building gave way to commercial and municipal structures. The first big block of factories was built by Youngs for Howlett & White, facing St. George's Plain when Mr. John Youngs was just 21 years old. Curiously enough the firm, in 1909, completed a further block, when his son, James, came of age. James Bernard Youngs, born 1888, has left eloquent testimony of his early days in the firm. *'Up-to-date machinery was not then available. Consequently, sawing, planing, mortising and moulding had to be done by hand. I had to fall into line with other tradesmen and was at work at 6.30 a.m. My wages for the first year were 3s. a week, rising to 10s. per week at the end of five years.'*

By 1910 the firm had completed a great number of buildings, many of which are still well known in the city. In particular, in July, 1884, work began to replace 'the cheerless, dismal, heterogeneous collection of shanties' (Thorpe Station), at a cost of £60,000. The work was completed in time for the official opening on 3rd May, 1886. The old Royal Hotel in the Market Place was pulled down and the site turned into one of the prettiest and up-to-date Arcades in the country; the building of the new Royal Hotel on Bank Plain costing £23,905, was completed in fifteen months.

Other landmarks included the Higher Grade Schools in Duke Street; the Training College in College Road, (later a victim of the bombs); a large chocolate factory for Messrs. A.J. Caley & Sons; The Grand Hotel at Cromer, and many other beautiful seaside Hotels, county Mansions and Halls, and also the Yarmouth Hippodrome.

In the years after the First World War, now directed by James (known as Jim or J.B.), they continued to build many memorable features of the Norwich skyline: notably the 300,000 gallon reinforced concrete water tower for Norwich Corporation. This progress was only temporarily impeded by a disastrous fire at the Chapel Field

Higher grade school for boys and girls opened in Duke Street in 1889.

premises, necessitating a move to City Road, where they took over the company and premises of the builders, J.S. Smith & Son.

During the Second World War the Youngs' works were severely damaged by enemy action. They conducted their business from wooden sheds on their bombed site and new premises were built on an enlarged site in 1947.

Youngs played a prominent role in the rebuilding of the city: Mackintosh's factory (and they have been working there ever since), Bonds in All Saints Green, and much of St. Stephens, rose again from the crumbling remains of war-torn Norwich, to become part of the new city. The new Wincarnis factory was built in Westwick Street. It was, together with a new furniture factory at New

The Norwich and Ely Training College for Schoolmistresses in College Road, built by Youngs in 1891.

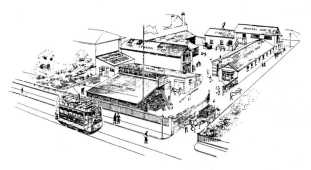

Premises of J.S. Smith, Norwich, taken over by Youngs & Son in 1927.

Mills Yard, one of the first barrel vaulted buildings to be erected in Norwich.

To mark their Centenary year in 1951 Youngs & Son held a dinner for their 350 employees at the Lido Ballroom in Aylsham Road, and a business Reception at the Assembly House. A B.B.C. concert, staged at the Lido to co-incide with their celebrations, starring Max Wall, Betty Huntley Wright and the Burt Twins, was recorded as a 'Workers' Playtime' and went out on the Midland Home Service.

By this time the firm had acquired a new Director, Michael John Youngs (b.1919), who joined the firm on leaving the army, where he had won the Military Cross and been mentioned in Despatches. It was he who guided the firm's post-war operations. In particular in the 1960s he decided that it was wasteful to have their own plant standing around idle. With the agreement of his Co-Directors he decided to set up a plant hire company. An old caravan was obtained and placed in front of the City Road Works. Morris Sillett, a young man working in the Costing Office, was asked to run it. He did a marvellous job, and from those humble beginnings evolved a Company that almost took over the site, and diversified and expanded. The boy from the Costing Office is now the Managing Director of a large company.

In 1967 John Youngs was incorporated within the R.G.Carter Group.

In 1970 they built Prospect House, home of Eastern Counties Newspapers, a new landmark for the city, on the site of the old Golden Ball public house; they were much involved with the Norfolk & Norwich Hospital, building the new Diagnostic and Treatment Ward, and continued working on the site for eleven years.

It was felt an opening existed for non-standard doors, and from 1971 these were produced in tandem with general joinery. The joinery side was phased out in 1977, to be superseded by a specialist unit, Youngs Doors. They are a highly specialist production unit, now a Limited Company, supplying most of the major contractors in the United Kingdom with non-standard flush doors, and orders have been obtained from many parts of the world including the supply of 120 doors, made from prime teak, inlaid with wood, brass and bronze, for the £600 million Kuwait Conference Centre.

Michael John Youngs, who retired from the building scene in 1972, was awarded an M.B.E. in the New Year Honours List. His father received the same honour exactly thirty years ago.

PERSONALITIES

It is very evident from the length of time that many employees have served this company, sons often following their fathers into the business, that it was a happy work place.

Mr. Leonard Dagless was General Manager of Palmers of Aylsham. James Youngs met him whilst attending the official opening of an extension at Paston School, and told him that if he ever wanted to change jobs he could join him at Norwich. Len joined the firm in 1945, just one week before Michael Youngs returned from the War, and at first lived in a house on the site at City Road Works. He was appointed General Manager and later became Contracts Director.

John Youngs met Robert William Trower on a railway station, and discovered that he too was in the building industry. He eventually came to Norwich to work for John Youngs as Chief Clerk. He became 'a genius at estimating'. Later his son Robert William junior, came into the business, and then David, his grandson, joined the firm when he left school, and worked at East Dereham. Later he was in charge of a subsidiary company at Bury St. Edmunds, before coming back to Norwich, and working under Leonard Dagless. When he retired David took over as, and still is, Director and General Manager of John Youngs (as part of the Carter Group).

Ronald T. Rule says he is 'a new boy'. A trained accountant, he was appointed Company Secretary nearly thirty years ago, and is now a Director of Builders Equipment (Norwich) Limited.

Two other personalities over the years were Basil Gooderham and John Cutting – both progressed from real 'Juniors' to Chief Clerk and Estimating Director. John Cutting joined the old firm in 1928.

On 23rd March 1951 an employee wrote to J. Youngs & Son as follows:-

Dear Sirs – I esteem it a great privilege of you giving me the invitation to come to your Centenary Event of Youngs & Son Builders and Contractors. It will be long remembered in years to come by all who was there at that gathering at the Lido. I think they all enjoyed themselves. I did – that was a good dinner with drinks – one of the best to be had. Thank you all for the same.

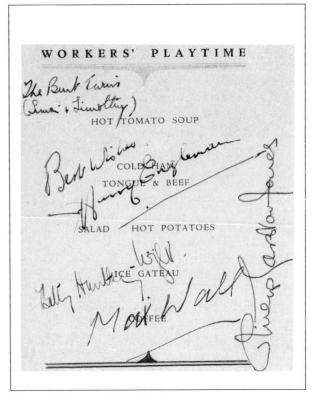

I started to work for the firm over 60 years ago in 1879 as a boy at 3 pence an hour – long hours them days too – we used to work longer hours – 64 a week. Money was 6d an hour for best men, 3d per hour for labourers. In them days houses were built in Bartholomew Close, Nelson Street for Watson, Heigham Hall – he used to give us beer – how many men – 20 all grades – 40 pints, two pints each. They worked then, no slacking, houses in Heigham Street built as well I work on all of them. Now we come to more houses in Stafford Street – a waste piece of ground there – new road were made there – rows of houses were built round these roads. I work on all of them being built by your father and grandfather. Now we come to Clarendon Road and Unthank Road. Nearly all the houses were built there all around them roads by J. Youngs & Son – I work on them.

Now we come to Chapelfield Road, the Chapel was erected there and houses as well. J. Youngs & Son give us employees all a good Outing to Yarmouth when we built the Chapel and paid for everything good. Now we come to Caleys, Coburg Street, the first factory being built there. Caleys gave all the men one pint of hot cocoa for breakfast every morning beside 3d a day and when the Factory was finished the men all of them were given a present of money – I done the carting there. Now we come to Noverres Rooms, Theatre Street. A job well done and carried out satisfactory to all concerned and they gave us all a good dinner and I was there and took part in it. Good people them days. Now we come to St. Stephens, Buntings, Curls, The Arcade, and the best of all, the Royal Hotel, a landmark,

pride of the city – I done the carting. Now Thorpe Station – I work there on the mortar mill. And now the Grand Hotel, Cromer – when complete John Youngs give us all a good dinner.

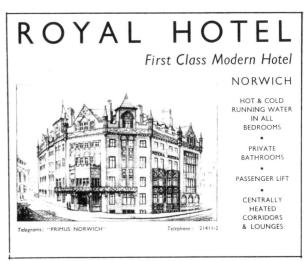

Advertisement for the Royal Hotel – 1951.
The architect was Edward Boardman.

Other large buildings were erected – Lowestoft Grand Hotel – they worked on nights with flares all round and goods yard at station blocked up with trucks of bricks – I was there carting, a great sight to be seen carts back and forwards with bricks. Halls were built all over the country in Norfolk and Suffolk and the Eastern Counties by J. Youngs & Son the well known firm for good work being done and carried out to the satisfaction of all concerned. Buildings have been built all over the city by J. Youngs & Son. They lead – others follow. Second to

Memorandum of Agreement

made the *nineteenth* day of *October* 18**96** between *The Royal Hotel, Norwich Limited whose registered address is "The Walk," Norwich* of the one part, and *John Youngs of Chapel Field, Road, Norwich, Builder* of the other part. **Witnesseth**, that the parties hereto hereby mutually contract and agree with each other; and the said CONTRACTOR, so far as the stipulations and provisions of this contract and the works, matters, and things herein mentioned or referred to, are to be performed and observed by him, hereby agrees with the said PROPRIETORS *and the said Proprietor* so far as the said stipulations and provisions, matters, and things, are to be performed by him, hereby agrees with the said CONTRACTOR as follows, namely :—

Parties to Contract.   1.—In the construction of these presents, when the Contract will admit of it, the term " Contractor " shall mean the said *John Youngs* ; the term " Proprietors " shall mean the said *The Royal Hotel Norwich, Limited* ; the term " Architects " shall mean MESSRS. EDWARD BOARDMAN AND SON or other the Architects for the time being employed by the proprietors to superintend the erection and completion of the works; and this term "works" shall mean all the works, acts, matters, and things specified and described in the specification, plans and other drawings, and detailed bills of quantities supplied, hereinafter mentioned, and also such other works, matters, and things as are hereby contracted to be done and performed by the contractor.

Material & Workmanship.   2.—The contractor shall well and substantially and in the best and most workmanlike manner, with the best materials of their respective kinds, and under the direction and inspection of the Architects and to their satisfaction in all respects, make, execute, finish and complete and deliver

Completion.   over to the proprietor, on or before the *Thirty-first* day of *October 1897* the several works, acts, matters and things mentioned or referred to in (or necessarily implied by) the specification, plans and drawings, or any of them, already prepared by the Architects, and

Time for Extras.   signed by the parties, and in the detailed bills of quantities supplied, with such additions, enlargements, and alterations of, and deviations from, the said works (if any), as the Architects may from time to time, during the progress of the works, direct; and in this respect time shall be

First page of the contract to build the Royal Hotel, Norwich for £23,095.

none in the city. I have had great experience in the building trade all my life – ups and downs I have had and I come out on top. I am well known in building trade during them years for my trade union and labour activities on the Building Trade Federation as a Delegate for years. I could write a lot more but I will conclude this letter now. Excuse me for mistakes made are many.

Now I wish you J. Youngs & Son Every Success and may your trade flourish for many years to come. God Bless you all.

This letter written by a man who must have been at least eighty years old, shows the pride and affection which this great family firm engendered in its employees.

The Royal Arcade, Architect: George Skipper. Built in 1889 on the site of what was, until 1841, The Angel, a famous old Norwich Inn. This was demolished and The Royal Hotel took its place. The Hotel frontage still remains at the entrance to the Arcade on The Walk.

H. RUMSEY WELLS

The firm of G. & S. Wells, Club, Regimental & School Outfitters, was established in Cockey Lane (now London Street) in 1815. This was at a time when sportsmen wore tall beaver hats to play golf, cricket or bowls, and for fishing, shooting and hunting. The only people who wore caps were schoolboys, and gamekeepers, who wore black or blue 'Melton' cloth caps with neck and ear flaps similar to the modern skiing cap.

Head measuring device used by Rumsey Wells.

Gamekeeper's Cap

Designed in 1830

Made in thick "Melton" cloth and Back-stitched by hand.

Thomas Wells, born 23rd June, 1841, and educated at the Model School in Princes Street, was, by 1879, senior partner in the firm of T. Wells & Son, who were manufacturing hats and caps for the wholesale and retail trade in a three-storey building at No. 19 St. Andrew's Hill. They

H. RUMSEY WELLS

Rumsey Wells wearing his grandfather's top hat, made in 1815.

MY caps are hand-cut from hand-spun and hand woven tweeds, *not* from what is known in the trade as "cap cloths," but the best products of England, Scotland and Ireland: they are hand-made by carefully trained girls in my own workrooms—they are lined (the caps, not the girls) with silk or satin—the peaks are made of specially compressed leather—the completed cap is a thing of beauty and a joy for ever.

EXTRACT FROM LETTER.

Rouen, 5th Jan., 1919.

"N'oubliez pas en venant la casquette que vous m'avez promise, la mienne est usée, après 36 nettoyages."

E. BOILLOT.

I am passionately fond of beautiful things, and endeavour to make my caps as beautiful as possible. I don't pretend that they are cheap, but I maintain that they are cheapest in the long run.

A customer of mine who lives in Holland told me the other day that when he was in Buenos Ayres 8 years ago, someone stole one of the caps that I had made for him. Of course, this demonstrates that there was at least one man in South America who knew a good thing when he saw it.

THE REEPHAM.

THE YARE.

THE BURGH

THE BLOFIELD.

THE WROXHAM.

THE PLUMSTEAD.

manufactured a wide variety of headgear and supplied best-class establishments throughout the country. Thomas Wells won many prize medals, and was the first maker of sporting caps suitable for hunting, racing, bicycling, boating, riding, smoking, shooting or travelling, and in all sorts of materials ranging from tweed or cloth to furs and velvets. They also made forage and other caps for the Services and supplied a large number of boating and other clubs, bands, etc. Thomas said 'The Hussars, at present stationed in Norwich, are excellent judges, and their officers are highly satisfied with the articles supplied to them from this establishment.'

Thomas had a son, Herbert Rumsey. Born in 1877 at Hellesdon, he became a partner in the business in 1904, by which time the firm had moved to No.4 St. Andrew's Street, whence issued forth a stream of advertising material promising caps and ties cut from handwoven material to order in the course of three hours. They also sold embroidered badges, club, school and regimental colours in ribbons, ties and sashes, clerical felt hats, birettas, and vestments from Norwich silk. When hats were made to order records of size and shape were kept for many years. One middle-aged man returning to Norwich after many years and wanting a new cap was amazed to find they still had the measurements for his school cap.

Rumsey Wells were not slow to introduce new styles into their headgear. Caps gradually became fuller in the front, at the sides, and eventually all round. With the advent of the motor car came the flat, circular-topped cap with its padded lining, and that is when Rumsey Wells got the chance to design his famous 'Doggie' caps which became known all over the world. The first were called the 'Brancaster' and the 'Blofield'. During the First World War he produced the first semi-soft service cap for officers, and after the war, the 'Westwick' and the 'Conesford'. He was quite a character, with elegant whiskers, fine hats, a cloak, and immaculate shirts and ties. Service, quality and humour were the trademarks of a business which, in 1935, was advertising its caps as the most expensive in the world. Rumsey said *'No other capmaker, except my grandfather and father, properly 'finished' a cap by putting a row of stitching at the edge of the cap. This finish is one of the distinguishing features of a 'Doggie' cap and enables it to be put on and raised from the head like a bowler hat.'*

An ingenious and indefatigable self-publicist,

Rumsey Wells wearing the "Watton" priced from 21s 6d. depending on material selected.

Rumsey liked to produce booklets and pamphlets extolling the virtues of his hats and caps and telling a little of the story of Norwich and its silk industry. In 1919 he wrote 'A customer, travelling overland from South Africa, arrived alone at Cairo, not knowing a soul. After a bath and change he put on his cap I had made for him, and took a walk. Seeing another man on the other side of the street, he walked up to him, clapped him on the back, saying 'I don't know who the blazes you are, sir, but you are wearing a Wells' cap, so dammit come and have a drink.' This little story is intended to convey the distinction occurring to men who invest in a Wells cap.

He died in 1937 but the business continued until 1974. The premises are now a public house but the name remains, and if you care to visit the Strangers' Hall Museum you can still see the sign depicting the three wells and the rising sun, for Wells & Son, which was a familiar sight outside the shop in St. Andrews for so many years.

MANN EGERTON & CO. LTD

In April, 1899, Gerard Noel Cornwallis Mann, a Cornishman, and an electrical engineer, happened to see from an advertisement that an electrical installation business in the city was for sale. He came to Norwich and bought it, taking over the existing premises at No.2 Redwell Street. The vendors were Laurence, Scott & Company, who had decided to concentrate on making machines and control gear, and were therefore selling off the substantial electrical contracting business they had built up. Their annual turnover was in the region of £5,000, and they sold the stock and goodwill of the business to Mr. G.N.C. Mann for £2,600. Laurence Scott undertook not to engage in contracting in Norfolk for five years, and many of their employees were retained by Mann. (One of them was still working for Mann Egerton thirty years later). Mann soon opened new showrooms across the street at the corner of Queen Street and Bank Plain.

Premises of G.N.C. Mann & Co. Electrical Engineers. Corner of Bank Plain and Queen Street.

Mr Gerard Noel Cornwallis Mann, founder of Mann Egerton & Co. Ltd.

In 1900 Mann took into partnership Hubert Wingfield Egerton, well-known for his early historical motoring exploits, including a trip from Lands End to John O'Groats in a 3.5 h.p. De Dion Bouton Voiturette. A none too easy task nowadays, but even more difficult in those early days of motoring. They started in the young motor trade in a very small way in premises at No. 5. Prince of Wales Road, which would hold two cars only in the showroom, and four in the works. The first car they sold was a Locomobile Steam Car. In the early days Gerard Mann often had to test cars himself, give trial runs, do hire work, and even assist in dismantling and erecting cars. Their floor space to begin with was under 1,000 sq. ft., and they had a staff of 10. (By 1928 they were advertising 230,000 sq.ft., which included several depots, and had a staff of over 850). Mann, Egerton & Company Limited was formed in 1905. By 1908 they were as agents for many manufacturers of cars, and were advertising garage accommodation for 200 cars. They also built up a 'used car' trade and gained quite a reputation for reliability both at home and abroad. They were shipping good used cars to a trader in New Zealand in the very early years of the century.

Despite the rapid development of their motor car interests, they also expanded as electrical engineers. There was ever increasing electrification of country houses, factories, churches and public buildings, and among the earliest contracts were installations for the Royal Naval Cordite Factory, Poole; Torpedo Ranges at Weymouth; Air Sheds at Pulham and War Office Camps on Mousehold.

Henry Royce and the Hon. Charles Rolls began their partnership in May, 1904, and today their joint names still symbolise excellence in motoring. Five years after the meeting of Royce and Rolls Mann Egerton began their close association with their firm. They had begun coachbuilding in 1901 and had established a reputation for good workmanship. They mounted their first body, a Landaulette, on a Rolls Royce chassis in 1909 at the Cromer Road depot. It was the beginning of a long line of Rolls Royce bodies made to customers' requirements by their coachbuilders and Rolls Royce officially

Interior of the garage at Prince of Wales Road, c. 1910
No 5 CL was owned by Mr. Mann.

recognised Mann Egerton bodies from the early 1920s.

A Trade Directory of 1910 shows:

Mann Egerton & Company Limited, 5 Bank Plain. Garage & Works Nos. 5 & 7 Prince of Wales Road; also at Ipswich and Lowestoft. Telegraph address ''Installation, Norwich''. Tel. Nos. 217 and 482.

It was about this time that Hubert Egerton severed

The first driving school in the country, c.1919: Note the two steering wheels.

his connection with the company.

1912 saw the erection of the greater part of the present day works, one of the first re-inforced concrete buildings in the country.

By 1913 they had branches throughout the Eastern Counties and in London. They became specialist coachbuilders – motor car buyers wanted individuality and superior workmanship. The chassis would be purchased from the manufacturers and the customer, in consultation with the company, would decide on the coachwork. Nothing was mass produced in those days. They had hundreds of cars of more than nine different makes, and regularly exhibited at Olympia.

They offered their customers:
"Free Delivery
One week's free tuition
Free tuition in our works for coachman
Payment by instalments, if desired"

Then came the First World War and in 1915 the Admiralty asked them to build aeroplanes. A War Loan of £30,000 enabled the company to acquire 60 acres of what was then open land on Cromer Road, Hellesdon. A huge wooden hangar was built, 200 ft. long and 100 ft. wide, with a superb 'bowstring' roof consisting of 20 enormous lattice arches. The building, which used up 70,000 sq. ft. of boarding,

was begun on 5th March 1916, and by the end of April planes were being constructed on the premises. They also constructed a triangular shaped flying field on what is now a residential area.

In order to cope with this work the whole of the extensive coachbuilding factory, as well as a large proportion of the motor repair and engineering works, were used for aircraft manufacture.

Ten separate and distinct models of aircraft were successfully produced, amongst which were numerous SHORT Bombers, SOPWITH 1½ Strutter Twin-seat Fighters, Single-seater French designed SPAD SCOUTs, DE HAVILLAND long range Bombers, and 184 SHORT Seaplanes. The size of the machines varied from 26 feet span to 86 feet span, and the horse-power from 110 to 800.

On a Saturday afternoon in September 1919, there was an unfortunate accident at the Aylsham Road aerodrome. A standard De Havilland aeroplane which had been taken over by, and was the property of the Government, failed to rise properly from the ground on starting to fly to Mousehold Aerodrome, with the result that it fouled the telegraph wires running along the Aylsham Road, crashed on to a field on the opposite side of the road, and was badly damaged. The Pilot, Lieutenant Dainty, RFC, and an RFC mechanic

Group taken in front of the first 110 Sopwith 1½ strutter fighter plane produced by Mann Egerton. Mr Mann is third from left on the back row.

were seriously injured and taken in a Police Ambulance to the Norfolk & Norwich Hospital, the two other occupants of the machine escaped with a shaking. A spectator of the accident stated that the pilot did not seem to attain the speed necessary to lift a machine of that size and weight from the ground.

With their staff of skilled engineers they also looked after the maintenance of thousands of tractors, so essential to the War Effort. Manufacture of aeroplanes ceased at the end of the war and Mann Egerton were left with a work-force of nearly 1,200 people, specialist plant, buildings and machinery. Shares were issued and they became a public company. They started to create custom-made furniture, and within ten years were regarded as being among the four leading designers and

A combined wireless set and writing desk, custom made by the Woodworking Department.

producers of educational furniture in the country. By the 1930s the manufacture of wireless cabinets was a major activity, an order for 4,000 being received. The old hangar was taken into use for several years, and later served as a store. It was demolished in 1984, a victim of redevelopment at the Cromer Road premises. As a consequence of the experience gained in the operation of tractors in Norfolk and Suffolk for the Food Production Department of the Board of Agriculture, a large Agricultural Department was set up, and agencies secured for the best tractors and implements. Large stocks were held and skilled engineers were employed to overhaul and repair tractors and other agricultural machinery.

At the Annual Meeting of the Company in 1920, the Managing Director, Mr. G.N.C.Mann, said that in the Prospectus which had been issued by the Company last December it had been stated that a profit of £39,000 was envisaged. The actual profit was one of £37,540. There had been a serious loss of business due to the miners' strike, an unexpected extension of excess profits duty from 40% to 60%, and a slump in business. He still thought the profits were satisfactory, and said the company now included depots in London, Ipswich, Bury St. Edmunds and Lowestoft. They had departments dealing with coach-building, commercial vehicles, electrical contracting work of all kinds, petrol air gas for lighting, heating and cooking, agricultural tractors and implements, the manufacture of various engineering specialities, and of school and office furniture, and the sale of products of Messrs. Vickers Limited, whose agency the company held for five counties. The Directors at that time were Mr. A.C. Shepherd, Capt. F.C. Vernon Wentworth, C.B., Mr. L.A.C. Cole, and Mr. H.E. Hughes.

By 1922 they were listed as electrical engineers at Nos.21 & 23 King Street and as motor car engineers at Nos.5,7 and 13 Prince of Wales Road, 25 King Street, and Greyfriars, Norwich, with the agricultural Motor Department at Nos.18-22 Prince of Wales Road. They built coaches to cater for the now popular 'seaside excursions' being taken by the mass of the population.

The *Eastern Daily Press* of 18th February 1928, reported on a dinner and social given by the Directors to the staff. 200 people attended at the Arlington Rooms, and dancing continued until 1 a.m., music being supplied by The Radio Dance Band, Mr. K.A.J. Varney, Secretary of the Company presided. Mr. Mann said 'It is our policy never to engage an outsider if there is any suitable individual already in the employ of the company whom we can promote.' It was said that there were always opportunities for individuals in the company because Gerard Mann's four children were not involved. There were no family interests, only Mr. Mann, and no controlling share interests.

This Mann Egerton built body on a Rolls-Royce chassis is a fine example of the work carried out in the 1920s and 1930s.

On 3rd November, 1934, a fierce fire broke out at Aylsham Road. Damage was estimated at £10,000. The main sawmill was gutted and some valuable machinery lost, but the remainder of the premises escaped the blaze. The Fire Brigade received the call, the first at their new Fire Station, at about 1.15p.m. and was in attendance until 7.30p.m., directed by the Chief Constable and Superintendent Scott.

Mann Egerton exhibited regularly at the London Motor Show until 1938. With the start of the Second World War they ceased their coach-building activities and once again became involved in producing vehicles for the Government, including ambulances and troop carriers. Some 4,000 vehicles were made and another 3,000 were renovated and repaired, and thereby kept in service. The first radar station in East Anglia was installed by Mann Egerton, and essential repairs to shipping in ports all over the country were carried out. The woodworking department is said to have made over half a million pieces of furniture for the Government, including school and office furniture to replace that destroyed in the blitz.

Gerard Mann, formerly of The Oaks, Harvey Lane, Norwich, and later of No.100, Newmarket Road, died in 1941, and therefore did not live to see the era of prosperity, and the expansion of his company after World War II. The car-owning population increased and there was an enormous demand for vehicles.

The woodworking department expanded their activities – supplying thousands of items to the London County Council, and other authorities and to universities. They fitted out laboratories, lecture theatres, civic centres, hospitals and hotels, and were awarded the main contract for the provision of shelving at the new Central Library, Bethel Street, Norwich.

The firm acquired more and more companies but the engineering works and goodwill were sold to the Westinghouse Brake & Signal Company in April, 1964. The former engineering works and the now vacant coachworks were converted into a vast specialised vehicle centre at Cromer Road.

In 1955, on a site in Surrey Street Street, once the secluded garden of St. Catherine's Close, a new depot was built. The building was flanked by rose gardens, with showrooms and workshops set back 35ft from the pavement. The showroom was erected with 184 ft. of window space, and elsewhere there were expanses of glass to enable the public to view how the motor vehicles were serviced in the completely modern workshops. The Ford Depot in King Street was transferred to these premises, and in 1960 an extension was built for commercial vehicle repair. This site is now part of the massive expansion plan for the Norwich Union in Surrey Street.

February, 1960, saw an order for 15,000 desks, all of one size, for senior pupils in London Schools. This was the biggest order for individual desks of one type the firm had ever received. The furniture department was by now employing 625 people.

The Chairman of the Company, Mr. W.A. Paton retired in November, 1962 after 42 years' service. He joined Mann Egerton as a pupil in 1920 and subsequently held various executive posts. He was appointed a Director in 1933. He served in the Army in both World Wars and was awarded an M.C. during the second war, and was twice mentioned in despatches. He retired with the rank of Lt. Colonel and returned to the Company as Director and General Manager in 1944. He became Managing Director in 1946 and Chairman in 1948.

It was in 1962 that Mann Egerton adopted the famous TERN IN FLIGHT symbol, to be used, always in black and white, on all vehicles, stationery and publicity issued by the company. They chose this graceful, neat, easily recognisable design because of the company's East Anglian connections and because several of the commoner forms of this attractive sea bird breed on the Norfolk coast.

A new Commercial Vehicle Centre was opened at Cromer Road, Hellesdon in March, 1965.

The *Eastern Evening News* of 11th September 1973 contained the following announcement: 'Inchcape & Company, a large public company with world-wide interests in commerce and industry have made an offer valued in excess of £17½ million for Mann Egerton, the Norwich based firm. Acceptance of the offer was recommended unanimously by the Directors. Mann Egerton are one of the leading motor distributors of British Leyland and Rolls Royce cars in the U.K., with substantial interests also in motor repair and contract hire. Other activities include the manufacture of contract furniture and electrical contracting.'

The following year Richard Hawksley resigned as Chairman. His widowed mother had paid the company £150 in 1934 for a three year pupilship during which time he did not receive a salary. He began in Norwich, and in 1949 was appointed Manager of the Bury St. Edmunds depot. By 1950 he was Company General Manager working at the Head Office in Norwich. He was appointed to the Board in 1951, became Managing Director in 1957, and took the Chair five years later. Since 1957 he had seen the expansion of the firms' ten depots in London and East Anglia, grow, by 1974, to 76 scattered throughout the country.

Succeeding him as Chairman was Mr. J.W.D. Campbell. He joined the firm in 1950 after serving as an Officer in the Royal Navy Air Branch from the age of 17. He was elected to the Board in 1961, became executive Chairman of the company's Contract Wood-working subsidiary from 1964 to 1970, and assumed responsibility for the firm's motor interests in 1971. He became sole Managing Director and Chief Executive of the Group in 1972. Jim Campbell himself retired as Chief Executive on 1st May, 1986, but continued as Non-Executive Chairman.

The Jaguar car operations were transferred to new showrooms and workshops at Cromer Road in October, 1986. The move, costing £500,000, created space at the company's Prince of Wales Road site, where the Austin Rover and Land Rover franchise remained.

The local newspaper reported in December, 1986, that the furniture business at Reepham Road was to be sold to its own management team. It was not anticipated that any of the 115 workers would lose their jobs or that major changes of policy would be made. This meant the end of Mann Egerton's involvement with all trades not directly related to the motor car industry.

Today the small business that started at the end of the last century still has its base on Prince of Wales Road, and there are magnificent showrooms, workshops, a petrol sales outlet, a tyre depot and a large vehicle leasing company.

In 1986 a new Mercedes Benz outlet in Coventry was named Gerard Mann, a fitting tribute to a great entrepreneur. Although now part of a huge company whose profits run into millions of pounds, they still retain the old traditions of good workmanship and customer satisfaction, and if you walk down King Street in Norwich, you can see examples of those gleaming, luxurious cars, whose company started their relationship with Mr. Mann and Mr. Egerton more than eighty years ago.

EASTERN DAILY PRESS — 31ST. OCTOBER, 1951
Motor Coach of Novel Design

CONSTRUCTIONAL ORDER FOR NORWICH FIRM by Our Industrial Correspondent.
Motor coach travel for private parties setting out with a common interest is likely to have future enjoyment enhanced by the revolutionary design of a new vehicle which has just been completed in Norwich. Hitherto, coaches for 50 or so passengers have generally meant the splitting up of the party on two decks, putting one section out of touch with the other on the journey. Now they can all be comfortably settled in one compartment, as a result of the successful development of a space-saving coach known as the Crennin-Duplex half-deck – Crennin being the name of the designer – for the

Novel bus design for a double decker bus built at the Cromer Road works.

construction of which Mann Egerton Limited have become the sole licensees.

The first of these compact, stream-lined coaches was driven from the firm's Cromer Road Works for tests on Mousehold a few days ago. Its unusual feature is the seating which puts the travellers in two tiers of seats within little more space than is required for a normal single-deck coach chassis. Passengers sit in fours, two facing two. Those above have equally comfortable accommodation.

The Norwich makers have laid down plans for the construction of 100 of these coaches in the first year and the development is one of no little interest to the many types of craftsmen involved in the skilled work. It means that a side of Mann Egerton activities which was prominent in the firm's programme before the war is being extended again and at the moment the demand for expert labour at the Cromer Road works is greater than the supply.

EASTERN DAILY PRESS — 20TH. DECEMBER, 1932
A Ride in a £5 Car (By a Correspondent)

I wonder if the prospect of a ride in a £5 car conjures up for you visions of a slow, jerky, bumpy, altogether ridiculous jaunt – seated much nearer

The £5 car at Rackheath Gates.

Heaven than one usually is in the cars of today – getting out and pushing up hills, getting in and holding on for dear life when going down – in fact, £5 worth of automobile that one might despair even of entering for the next 'Old Crocks' Race.

That, at any rate, was the vision conjured up by an advertisement which appeared in the 'Daily Press' where secondhand cars were offered from £5 to £1,200 in a year-end clearance sale by Mann Egerton.

Thinking I'd have a bit of fun at their expense – off I went to their showrooms, and asked for a trial run in the £5 car. The car was of quite good appearance, in fact, a 1925 Fiat two-seater. Its very respectable hood was up, the green paintwork was good, and although the coachwork and interior woodwork was certainly shabby, it still bore evident signs of initial good quality, and I'm sure that a little polishing cream would work wonders even now. We made a lively start off the car park into Prince of Wales Road, into Riverside Road, and then chugging up the various hills and twists and turns of Gilman Road. Then through to Heartsease Lane and via Plumstead Road into Rackheath village, past Rackheath Gates on to the Sprowston Road. There were three of us – the driver, myself and the staff photographer with his impedimenta – all comfortably accommodated. All this time the little car behaved splendidly – and when we got on to a good bit of road the speedometer (for it had one – and a clock too) registered up to 40! The brakes were responsive, as we found once when we inadvertently turned onto the wrong road.

Returning via Magdalen Street, the little Fiat was as well behaved in traffic as when she had the whole road to herself. I wondered how its performance would have compared with the £1,200 Rolls Royce also advertised – and I almost decided to ask for a trial run in that also – but my courage failed me! But I'm open to wager it would not have been 250 times better!

THE BOMBER BREAKS THROUGH

'The Bomber Breaks Through' was a water colour painted for us by Joseph Simpson. It showed a dog-fight between a First World War British bomber – a De Havilland 9 two-seater built by Mann Egerton – and five enemy fighting Scout 'planes.

The bomber was returning from a raid and was cut off from the lines by the Scouts. The pilot made straight for the leader who went down and crashed. The others broke formation and our bomber flew through this opening. A further 'plane was shot down and another damaged. Our bomber had been badly shot about and the tail severely damaged. Combat was, therefore, broken off and our bomber returned home.

MANN EGERTON & CO. LTD

The D.H.9 was No. D.1715, delivered by us on the 25th May 1918 and the pilot who flew on this mission on the 10th June 1918 was Captain Gordon Fox Rule of the Royal Flying Corps.

In 1921 Captain Fox Rule wrote to Mr. Mann asking if he could purchase the painting from us. A price was agreed by the Board but Captain Fox Rule was unable to raise the necessary sum so that painting remained with the Company. Over the years copies were made but the original was lost. It was discovered in a flooded cellar, completely sodden and beyond restoration.

What a pity Captain Fox Rule was unable to purchase it in 1921.

(When this aircraft was ready for delivery, on 25th May, 1918, a flying demonstration was given by Mann Egerton at their Cromer Road aerodrome, to which employees were invited. At the end of the demonstration the machine was flown to Mousehold with Mr. G. N. C. Mann as passenger.)

March 1988

Marie Lee
Archivist
Mann Egerton & Company Limited

R.J. READ LTD.

Milling is an ancient industry in this rich agricultural county of Norfolk and Roman and Saxon millstones can be seen preserved in our local museums. Windmills were a prominent feature in the landscape and in the last century could still be seen clustered around the city. The windmill gradually took the place of the watermill and these, in turn, gave way to the steam mill. With the introduction of roller milling many small steam mills ceased to manufacture flour and those that were left were enlarged.

Bread has always been an important register of social distinction. In medieval times when white flour demanded an expensive milling and sieving process, the poor ate brown bread and the rich ate white. As mechanization and technology improved the processes white bread became cheaper. Today the trend has been reversed and more people are eating granary and wholemeal bread, but fine white flour is still much in demand for bread-making and for baking.
The milling tradition in Norwich flourishes in the firm of R.J. Read Ltd. at the City Flour Mills in King Street.

The founder of the firm, Robert John Read, was born at Wrentham, Suffolk in 1851. He spent several years working in other flour mills before buying Ingate Mills, Beccles, in 1875. An honest, shrewd and hardworking man, a sportsman, Free Churchman and Councillor, he had to cope with gales and many other difficulties in his early years. By dint of hard work his business prospered and in 1889 it seemed prudent to expand the property.

The time was propitious. Roller milling had just been invented, which meant that fine white flour could be produced in great quantities by steam or electric power. He therefore installed a four-sack capacity plant by Whitmore & Benyon of Wickham, in a new building. His troubles were not over, however, for in March, 1895, there was a great gale and the mill chimney was blown down, and just one year later the whole mill was completely destroyed by fire.

Faced with a run of disastrous circumstances which might have daunted a lesser man, Robert John persevered. He found alternative premises in Westwick Street, Norwich, near the site of New Mills, (the old mills that had straddled the River Wensum for 500 years, and which were used in medieval times for milling, and later for pumping water and sewage). He purchased a flour mill, the property of John Lee Barber (who founded a business in Great Yarmouth, later owned by Reads). Once settled in Norwich the trade again expanded and he found himself having to acquire other premises to house stables for the horses that pulled the mill wagons. The production of self-raising flour began in 1906.

Still the elements conspired against him, specifically in the great Norwich flood of 1912. Six inches of rain fell in twelve hours, accompanied by a violent gale. Within 24 hours the rainfall had reached 7.34 inches and the low-lying parts of the city were under threat. The quiet meandering River Wensum became a thundering, crashing torrent, taking all before it, bursting its banks, destroying bridges, and spreading over the streets. In factories and houses along the banks of the river work had to stop and thousands were thrown out of employment. Read's mill and boiler house were under nine feet of water, sacks of meal and flour were ruined, tools and implements floated about in the water and a model bakery which had been erected to supply bread to the Army on manoeuvres was partly washed into the river.

Robert John Read continued milling throughout the First World War. It was during this period that a crankshaft broke and an electric motor was installed. It proved so efficient that electric drives were installed and steam was no longer used.

Robert died on 3rd October 1920, and the business became a Limited Liability Company on 28th June. 1921. The first Directors were his two sons, Robert John Read, junior (known as Jack), and Lewes Hector Read, together with F. G. Turner, who had been working in the business since 1901.

Several factors led the directors to look for other premises. For a start, seagoing coasters found their way to the site impeded by the bridges (look at the height of Bishopbridge and you will see why). At the same time there were opportunities for the import of grain by transhipment from the Continent in the newly developed motor coasters, rather than by transhipment into wherries or lighters at Great Yarmouth. They found what they wanted in King Street; a mill, with a large river frontage and wharves large enough to enable sea-going vessels to discharge their cargoes.

The Albion Mills, as they were called, had started life as a yarn mill in the 1830s. Robert John Read purchased the now derelict buildings of the Albion Mills Estate for £5,750, the conveyance being dated 14th May, 1932.

Expansion now beckoned, as sea-going vessels could serve the mill and Reads could develop their trade with imported grain. New buildings and plant were constructed, and a space on the wharf surplus to requirements was leased to R. Coller & Sons Ltd., coal and coke merchants.

Amongst the new imports were cargoes of oyster shell, brought in for the chicken/hen trade, and maize from Argentina. A maize flaking plant was erected in June 1932 and soon their well-known brand of 'Recero' flaked maize, advertised as 'the best for milk production and feeding all kinds of stock', was known throughout the country. The plant soon doubled its production, and within two years it had been quadrupled. A 1,000 ton silo was erected between the maize mill and the flour mill, and a new ten sack milling plant was installed in the main building. Another 1,000 ton wooden silo was erected to deal with English wheat.

Mr. F.G. Turner was succeeded by Richard Lee Barber, as Director in 1942. It was his father who had sold the Westwick Street site to the first Robert John Read.

The mill sustained only minor damage in the war, and they were able to continue working seven days

ROBT. JOHN READ'S
Superior Roller Flours

Are Milled from the Choicest Wheats grown and stands unsurpassed for all uses.

City Flour Mills, Norwich.

READ'S SPECIALITIES :
SELF=RAISING FLOUR
AND
"COUNTRYSIDE" WHEAT MEAL.

They are the Apex of Perfection.

Packed in small linen Bags and sold by all Grocers and Bakers.   A Booklet of Recipes in each Bag.

City Flour Mills, Westwick Street. Advertisement from
"Citizens of No Mean City", 1910.

a week in order to maintain the vital supplies of flour. The old mill in Westwick Street was not so fortunate. In 1942 that part of Norwich once more became a disaster area. Huge blocks of property were destroyed by heavy explosive and incendiary bombs. An observer next morning described the mill as just a smouldering outline of the original three storey building, etched against the skyline, merely girders and tangled wreckage to show where it had stood.

The Albion Mills, King Street, c.1900.

Floods in Westwick Street — August 1912.

Additional property was purchased after the war and a new office block was erected. Owing to the marshy condition of this riverside site it was necessary to use sixteen reinforced concrete piles for the foundations.

The firm took on another family member in the shape of Bryan C. Read, only son of L. Hector Read, who had graduated from Cambridge with a B.A. in Engineering. He worked in mills in England and Ireland before joining the family business in 1947. He is a keen yachtsman and took part in the Olympic trials at Torbay in 1948.

The next forty years saw the development of the business in four directions: The Norwich grain importing business expanded with the growth of the animal feed compounding industry and the demand for imported maize. At one time they were

The Mill site in King Street. Photograph taken from the top of Normandie Tower.

importing 1,000 tons a week by coaster during peak periods. This trade ceased after Great Britain joined the Common Market and home-grown cereals such as wheat and barley became relatively cheaper. The John Lee Barber business at Great Yarmouth was expanded and became one of the first companies to handle soya bean meal in bulk. The seed and grain business of John Lee Bennett, Downham Market was purchased. In 1965 the Woodrow flour business was merged with Reads, and became R.J.Read (Holdings) Ltd. and Read Woodrow Ltd. From then onwards all production was concentrated at the City Flour Mills (the former Albion Mill).

Today wherries no longer ply along the rivers of Norfolk to service the trading industries of Norwich. Reads were one of the last firms to use river transport but now rely on a modern fleet of lorries and tankers to take their products all over the country. No maize is imported and the maize trade has ended. They now concentrate entirely on flour milling. The mill in 1934 produced ten sacks an hour (one and a quarter tons). The mill in the same building today produces five tons an hour.

HILLS & UNDERWOOD
Distillery and Vinegar Works

During the 18th and 19th centuries more than a dozen firms were making vinegar in Norwich and there are many references to 'vinegar yards' in the city leases. The Norwich Vinegar Works and Gin Distillery of Messrs. Hills & Underwood were situated in Prince of Wales Road/Recorder Road and were the largest of the kind in East Anglia. They were established in 1762 but their original site is not certain.

It is thought the business was started in 1762 by Francis Gostling, a merchant of Duke's Palace Yard. A 1782 directory shows him as Distiller, Rectifier, Brandy and Vinegar Merchant, St. Faith's Lane. In 1802 his is listed as having a Vinegar Yard in St. Faith's Lane.

In 1817 Squire & Hills, Liquor Merchants, of Queen Street, took over the business, and this firm later became known as Hills & Underwood. In a brochure produced at the end of the last century they mention a foundation in 1762 when a small manufactory for vinegar was built on a site next to what was later to become the Prince of Wales Road, and that the business increased until it covered a wide area. It may be that vinegar companies were operating in several areas and that, with amalgamations, they came together as this large company in Prince of Wales Road.

The spirit of mid-Victorian expansion loomed large and a new factory was built in 1865 covering 125,000 square feet, with river frontage. The property included offices, fermenting rooms, vat stores, gin stills, spirit stores, boilers and warehouse facilities and, in common with the breweries, Hills & Underwood had their own cooperage. They were very proud of the fact that an ancient stone bridge belonging to the Greyfriars' Friary was on their site, and mentioned it in many of their advertisements.

The early manufacturing processes are well documented. Making vinegar was very similar to making beer, despite the absence of hops. The fine Norfolk malts were ground to a meal and placed in mash tuns. Here the meal was mixed with hot water and heated to boiling point. The wort was then cooled and placed in fermenting vats, yeast was added and alcohol was produced. This had to be converted to acetic acid; achieved by exposing the liquid to air. At one time this was carried out by vats in open-air vinegar yards but later processes were invented whereby the liquid was slowly trickled over birch twigs, the long exposure to air meaning that acidification could be achieved in 48 hours instead of the lengthy period of three months taken by the open-air method.

A CHEAP TOILET VINEGAR. When travelling or on a sea voyage the washing water often has a very disagreeable smell. To remove this a little toilet Vinegar should be put in it. A cheap and easy way of making this is as follows: Take a quart of brown vinegar, and in it place half a pound of fresh lavender. Let this soak for two weeks, then strain through a muslin bag.

Subsequently the vinegar had to be 'cleaned' and 'clarified', the resultant fresh malt vinegar being a pale primrose colour. Most customers preferred a darker colour, so caramel was added. This did not alter the taste but merely changed the appearance.

The size and number of the vats reminded visitors of those in the great breweries. They ranged in capacity from 11,500 to 27,000 gallons and were stretched in long lines almost touching the roof of the large storage building.

British Cordials, Liqueurs and the 'Celebrated Old Tom Gin' were also manufactured. Thousands of casks were exported annually.

In 1911 the firm was incorporated with that of Sir Robert Burnett & Company Limited and the works were closed down. The last of the buildings was demolished in the 1960s.

ADVERTISEMENT

BOTTLED VINEGARS: These may be had brown, pale, sherry, or straw coloured, or distilled (White Vinegar) as required, with the guarantee of the Maker's Label & Seal, as bottled at their works.
USES FOR VINEGAR SUGGESTED BY HILLS & UNDERWOOD: For lamp wicks of all kinds. Soak the wick in HILLS & UNDERWOOD'S Vinegar, and then thoroughly dry it before use. The result will be a beautifully bright light.

FOR CYCLISTS. Cyclists often complain of their lamps smoking and want a remedy. Dip the wick in vinegar for a few hours and allow it to dry. It will never smoke after this.

CRESS VINEGAR. Dry and pound half an ounce of cress seed. Pour upon it a quart of vinegar and let it steep for ten days, shaking it up every day. This is very strongly flavoured with cress, and with salads and cold meats is a great favourite with many.

SALAD DRESSING. Half a pint of best vinegar, 2 ozs. olive oil, yolks of three eggs, 3 grains of cayenne pepper, 2ozs. brown sugar, 1 ozs. mustard, 1 oz. salt, 3 ozs. clotted cream.

VINEGAR FOR HICCOUGH, &C. For hiccough it is the best of all known remedies. A teaspoonful will immediately allay the most violent attack of hiccough. With infusion of sage it forms a most excellent gargle in all cases of sore or relaxed throat.

Hills and Underwood's offices.

Hills & Underwood's Gin and Spirit Warehouse, Norwich.

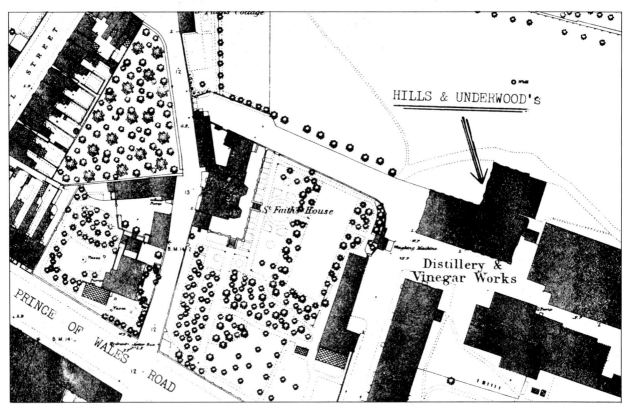

Ordnance Survey Map 1885.

FOR SPRAINS AND BRUISES. For sprains and bruises, where the skin is not broken, a lotion should be made with equal quantities of vinegar and warm water, and the part thoroughly fomented and wrapped in flannel which has been saturated with this solution.

VINEGAR FOR VETERINARY PURPOSES. Vinegar is much used for cracked heels in horses and for swellings, especially on the legs. In all sloughing wounds it acts as a most healing as well as a most powerful antiseptic agent. The strongest vinegar is best used for these purposes. An excellent stable lotion for general use may be made from equal parts of best vinegar and linseed oil.

VINEGAR FOR COUGH MIXTURE. Boiled with honey it forms a most excellent and effective Cough Mixture, especially for children. A pound of honey, half a pint of vinegar, and a quarter of pint of water should be boiled and stirred until the honey is dissolved. Dose: For children a teaspoonful, for adults a tablespoonful, taken frequently.

PANKS ENGINEERS

Characteristically, the Victorian entrepreneur was a rural man who moved townwards in the great mid-century migration. In 1842 Abraham Pank left his native village of Bawburgh, with his wife and Richard, his small one year old son, to set up business in Norwich as a brass worker, gas fitter and bell hanger. His first premises were at No. 100 and later No.123 Pottergate, but in 1858 he purchased property in Bedford Street for £525, and in 1874 further adjoining property was acquired for £640. Both properties were inherited by Richard in 1877, and he, in turn, left the properties to his three sons Richard Arnold, Abraham and Arthur Robert. (He also had four daughters, Connie, Mollie, Henrietta and Clara). In the Norwich Postal Director of 1879 the entry shows:

PANK & SON. Gas engineers and fitters, bell hangers and metal workers, lamp, beer-engine, bath and hot water apparatus manufacturers, ventilating and sanitary engineers, Bedford Street, St. Andrews.

When Abraham, the second son, reached the age of 15 (1885) he was apprenticed to Richard Robert Riches and Charles James Watts, Gas Engineers and Fitters. A hundred years on his indentures make interesting reading. His father had to pay a premium of £100 in four instalments, and Abraham received a weekly wage of 4s. for the first year, 6s. for the second, 8s. for the third, and 10s. for the fourth. On the 5th year the Indenture papers stated that he would work in the Drawing Department under the personal instruction of Mr. Watts but would not receive a wage. He worked long hours, starting at 7 a.m. on Mondays, but at 6 a.m. on the other days. He finished at 5 p.m. except on Saturdays, when he left at 2 p.m. He was allowed half an hour for breakfast, and an hour for lunch, except on Saturdays when he merely had the half-hour break. During this period Abraham still found time to get married to Ethel Heyhoe, a girl of eighteen whose father was in charge of prisoners at the Bridewell. By 1900, the year his apprenticeship ended, they had a daughter Kathleen, and a son Herbert. Later

three more children were born: Philip (who became a Quantity Surveyor: the firm, Philip Pank & Partners, still continues in Norwich and London), Betty (who married a Mr. Brett), and John. Kathleen, their first born, married a Mr. Larking. After finishing his apprenticeship Abraham, now a fully qualified engineer, went to sea, firstly in the 'North Tyne' and in 1891/2 in the 'Congo'.

By 1896 Kelly's Directory shows that Panks had extended their field of operations:

A PANK & SON. Gas, electric light and sanitary engineers, drain testers, plumbers, electric bell, telephone and gas fitters, medieval and general metal workers, contractors to H.M.Office of Works, district agents for Crossley gas and oil engines. Nos. 8, 10 & 12, Bedford Street.

In 1902 Panks gave public proof of their growth by purchasing the old established firm of Holmes & Sons, Agricultural Implement Makers and Engineers, of Prospect Place Works. Mr. F.R. Holmes had died and the business had been discontinued, although unfortunately much of the equipment and machinery had already been disposed of. Panks purchased the goodwill of the business in 1902 but did not buy part of the property on Castle Hill until 1906. Pank & Son would continue to manufacture and supply the various machines and duplicate parts for their engines, turbines, pumps, machines, implements, etc. as hitherto made by Holmes. Panks informed their customers that they had a staff of first-class engineers, including Mr. W. Stringer, who had for many years been Foreman Engineer to Holmes & Sons.

By 1905 Richard Arnold had moved to Great Yarmouth and opened branches in Howard Street, Albany Road and Southtown. (The Howard Street business continued until the last war, the property finally being sold in 1946).

In the years after the First World War the firm made several significant moves. They purchased the goodwill of the firm of Riches & Watts, Engineers. In 1926 they started an auto-electrical department.

In 1929 they purchased Messrs. C. & E. Gates, Electrical Engineers, and moved the central heating, electrical installation and refrigeration departments to No.29 St.Giles Street, under the control of Clifford, son of Arthur Robert, who was joined by his brother Michael in 1940. Meanwhile, Herbert and John took an active part in the Norwich firm and in 1929 Herbert took over the engineering side of the business, and John the Radio, opening a branch at Orford Place.

As technology improved, electrical and engineering firms had to diversify to survive. By 1933 Panks were advertising themselves as agricultural, electrical, wireless, mechanical, heating engineers and contractors, mill furnishers and church furnishers, providing electric lighting for country houses, and were official repairers of C.A.V. batteries, and district agents for Crossley's gas and oil engines, at Nos. 8, 10 and 12 Bedford street, (Tel.No.100), and No. 24 Cattle Market Street, (Tel.No.60), wireless goods depot No.29 St. Giles Street. The Engineering department were heavily engaged in maintenance work at the Pockthorpe Brewery of Steward & Patteson.

Bedford Street premises of A. Pank & Son. Richard Abraham Pank is standing in front of the window. The western half was purchased in 1858 for £525 and the eastern half in 1874 for £640. The property was sold to Curls in 1944.

By 1944 the Bedford Street premises had been sold to Curl Brothers for £10,000, a large sum of money in those days, and work was concentrated on the Castle Hill Works which housed modern electric and acetylene welding apparatus and possessed a well-equipped machine shop. The installation and maintenance of pumping plant and water supplies were a speciality, and well-boring and tube-driving was carried out by members of the firm's own labour force. The branch at St. Giles, alternatively, dealt largely with wireless installations and housed a staff of service mechanics who specialised in all radio repairs.

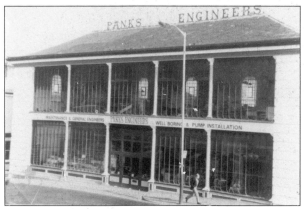

Cattle Market Street premises.

Plainly, there were limits to diversification. The firm operated as one company until 1950, although trading on several different sites. It was then split into A.Pank & Son Limited, Panks (Castle Hill) Limited, and Panks (Radio) Limited.

Panks Electrical carried out many large contracts: They undertook the wiring at Felbrigg Hall and a Luminous Indicator Call System was installed throughout the whole of the Norfolk & Norwich Hospital, whereby any number of persons, up to a total of 90, could be informed by flashing silent indicators that they were required. A similar system was installed at the Technical College on Ipswich Road.

Elsewhere, at Boundary Park Greyhound Stadium, Panks undertook the first installation of floodlighting in the area to enable football to be played after dark.

In these years heating and lighting contracts were carried out at Norwich City College gymnasium, and also for the Norwich Maddermarket Theatre. Many and varied were the contracts awarded to Panks of Norwich, they included boilers and central heating plant for the Norwich Union, and for private houses, re-tubing of large loco type steam boilers, farm water supply systems, boreholes, pumps, work at maltings, factories, houses and shops. At Christmas 1953, Mr. Alec Petitt retired. He had been with the firm since 1904.

Clifford's son William entered the business in 1961, and was later joined by Michael's son Timothy.

Meanwhile, Panks Radio, run by John Pank and his son Richard, who joined him in 1953, saw the demand for records, record players and radiograms increase, and the radio business expand – and with the coming of television, in 1954, a vast volume of business came into existence. By 1967 they had shops at Orford Place, Davey Place and No.105 Prince of Wales Road. They now operate from a shop in Anglia Square opened in 1970, with a Service Department at No.29 St.Giles Street.

A footnote to the history of the firm was provided by an event in April, 1974 when Waters & Son, Auctioneers, of Acle, announced a sale at The Foundry, Acle, of important millwrights' and foundry equipment, including about 1,000 19th century patterns, a steam engine, a millwright's old fire boiler, and heavy engineering equipment belonging to the firm of Smithdales. Peter Pank, who joined his uncle Herbert in 1960, and is now head of the Engineering Company, is a keen historian, very interested in the history of the City and of his company. He went to the auction and managed to purchase several interesting items, formerly the property of Holmes & Sons. One of them, a wooden pattern with the name 'Holmes, Engineers' he now keeps at the works. He says that when purchased the pattern was embossed with brass letters but unfortunately, when collected, these had been removed.

With an expanding company and parking difficulties in the City centre, Panks Auto-Electrical decided to look for other premises. They purchased property on the south side of Heigham Street which had been an old cigarette warehouse, demolished the ruins of 14 cottages and built new workshops. And then in 1982 the Old Tannery on the opposite side of the road came onto the market. It was an excellent opportunity to acquire 1½ acres just outside the old city walls, and Panks were delighted to make the move. They took with them to Heigham Street the attractive, ornate cast-iron lettering that had surmounted the Castle Hill premises.

Currently the firm in Heigham Street is divided into two parts. One side is auto-electrical, and the other engineering, dealing with a wide variety of business ranging from large contracts for pumping equipment for North Sea oil rigs, to models and model kits for engineers. Because Mr. Peter Pank had become more and more involved with engineering, he brought in a skilled Manager, Mr. Martin Pilgrim, to help on the auto-electrical side, and Mr. Pilgrim has now joined the board, of which Mr. Peter V. Pank is Managing Director, having taken over when his uncle Herbert died in 1970. The other members are his wife Ruth, and Mr.J.G. Larking, son of Kathleen Pank and Mr. G. Larking.

Panks Engineers have built up a reputation for skill, knowledge, understanding and personal service over five generations. At the Royal Norfolk Agricultural Show in 1983, 18 of the 24 vintage

Moving the letters – July 1983. From left to right – Peter Pank, Dick Betts, Ted Reed, Norman Moon and Barbara Francis.

Photo: Eastern Counties Newspapers.

engines on display carried their repair mark. They deal with garages, boatyards and motorists – and with car parking now made easy Mr. Pank says 'people often pop in during their lunch hours'.

The proximity of the Broads means that there is a lot of boatyard repair work, wiring, fault-finding, and working on the big hire fleets. They also supply the boat building industry, mainly luxury yachts, hire craft, and engine marinisers, with a whole range of equipment, from navigation lamps to solar power units. On the auto-electrical side they carry a stock of some 12,000 part numbers, and their reference library, going back fifty years, is what you would expect to find in this old established family business; augmented, however, by a computerised stock system. In common with many other successful local family businesses they employ many long-serving members of staff, all of whom are friendly, helpful, and willing to share the history of 'their firm' with others.

JOHN COPEMAN & SONS LTD
Wholesale Grocers & Provision Merchants

John Cozens, the 20 year old son of a farmer of Westwick, near North Walsham, and brother-in-law of Jonathan Davey (who built Davey Place in 1812), came to Norwich in 1789. With the assistance of Jonathan Davey he bought Newman's old established wholesale and retail grocery business on Gentlemen's Walk, and for a time the business was known as Cozens and Davey. By 1801 business had increased and takings were about £400 a week, three quarters of which was income from the wholesale trade.

Accounts books of the period make interesting reading, with references to hogsheads of sugar, puncheons of molasses, sperm oil, whale oil and other oil in casks, soap, tea, hops, coffee, cheese and a limited range of dried fruits, not forgetting snuff in bladders. There were very few of today's proprietary brands, most of the goods came in very large packages, or sacks. Road transport was difficult and hazardous and most goods were therefore brought in by trading wherries up the river from Yarmouth.

Jonathan Davey relinquished his share of the business in June, 1792, and John Cozens appears to have prospered despite the steady decline in the

A sketch by Miss Harriet Copeman of the original premises on The Walk c. 1810, then known as Cozens & Copeman.

41

JOHN COPEMAN & SONS LTD.

local weaving trade and the consequent unemployment of many skilled workers.

John Copeman, who gave the firm his name, was born in 1778 at Horstead He first appears in the accounts in 1802 when he was paid £1. By 1804 the books show that he had money in the business, and by the end of March, 1809, he had been made a full partner, the firm becoming Cozens & Copeman. John Copeman's wife had died earlier and he married Cozens' wife's sister, Elizabeth Hawkins. Trade grew and by the early part of the 19th century profits had reached around £1,000. It was important to secure the future of the business and in 1827 John and Elizabeth's son, John the Younger, was apprenticed to a grocer in Martham for four years, his father paying a premium of £60. At the end of his training the son joined the father's business, often travelling by coach to different parts of the country to sell their products. When Cozens retired in 1837 the father and son became partners and changed the name of the firm to Copeman & Son. They enlarged the buildings and installed a new shop front and rolling shutters. Another son, Jonathan Davey Copeman, also became a partner, but he left in 1847 to seek his fortune elsewhere.

John Copeman jnr. married in 1849, and two years later Henry John Copeman was born. John's father died in 1866, aged 87, and he became sole proprietor.

It appears that the wholesale side of the business became more and more important and in 1873 the retail premises at No.21 The Walk were sold to Charles Underhill & Company. At around the same time further alterations and improvements were made to the wholesaling building and in 1874 Henry John Copeman was admitted to full partnership with his father. Two years later Copemans were registering their brand names of 'Copeman's Parisian Coffee' and 'Royal Exhibition Coffee', said to have been the first coffee packed in tins. 'Star Baking Powder' also made its appearance, and the firm registered an eagle device which adorned their cheques until the 1940s.

In 1884 Henry Charles Laycock joined the firm as an office boy at a salary of 4s. per week. For all the innovation of the Victorian era, there had been little alteration in the conditions of the grocery trade. The company's travellers were called 'riders', a reminder of the fact their journeys were carried out on horseback. Goods were still being received in bulk. The hogsheads of sugar had to be dug out with a shovel, the dried fruit was rough and was 'dressed' by hand in a wire bottomed sieve, and syrup came in 12 to 14 cwt. puncheons. Long hours were worked, especially during the Christmas period. Office hours were 9 a.m. to 7 p.m. with a 'half day' which started at 5 p.m. on Thursdays. Local transport was by two-wheeled carts, which

Goods entrance, Castle Street.

were used to deliver orders in the city, and to carriers at the Inns who would transport the country orders, which had to be packed in stout boxes or casks to withstand the rigours of the rough journeys. Mr. Henry Copeman would journey once a year to Holland to buy Edam and Gouda cheese, and a butcher was employed for boning and rolling the meat.

In 1895 Charles Copeman, son of Thomas Parker Copeman and nephew of John became a partner. He

were encouraged to continue this work in other parts of the country. They diversified into other commodities, dealing with such items as beer, tobacco, cigarettes, vegetables, cake, kippers and sausages, and Mr. Laycock was made responsible for ordering the goods and seeing they arrived in good order and on time. The Army Canteen Committee eventually took over, but Copeman & Sons were at one time supplying rations and running canteens for 30,000 troops.

The Sale Room.

had been with the firm since leaving school fifteen years earlier and had travelled extensively for them.

John Copeman's death in 1899 at the age of 87 marked the end of an era.

By this time it had become apparent that larger premises were required and these were purchased adjoining Davey Place and Castle Street. Mr. Laycock, the warehouse manager organized the transfer of the firm's stock, something like 200 tons, to temporary buildings in Bethel Street, no easy task using horse-drawn vehicles. They moved to their new premises in 1903, and now had extensive cold storage equipment, an electric lift, a spacious loading dock and custom made offices.

The First World War brought obvious challenges to the grocery trade. Shortly after its commencement the War Office requested the company to supply rations for part of the first expeditionary force being assembled in North Norfolk. They organised canteens for army units stationed around Norwich so successfully that they

On 6th June 1917 a private company perpetuating the name of the first Copeman in the firm, was incorporated, called John Copeman & Sons Limited, with the two cousins Henry and Charles as sole directors. They were joined in 1921 with the appointment to the Board of Charles' brother John Lacy Copeman, and William Oliver Copeman, a son of Charles, who was a chartered accountant. Subsequently Mr. J.W. Longstaffe was also a director for a few years.

Mr. Charles Copeman died in 1925, on the day after the birth of his grand-daughter, the first of a new generation of Copemans.

The inter-war years brought fluctuating fortunes for the firm. John died in 1935, aged 83, and Mr. Longstaffe departed, leaving Henry and William as sole directors; but they were joined in 1936 by Charles Laycock, who had by then served the company for fifty years, and by Clifford Copeman Makins, a nephew of the Chairman. The General Strike, the increase in motor transport, the availability of a greater range of imported goods, all had an effect on the company, but they survived and prospered, maintaining the traditions of reliability, good quality and value for money, begun in the 18th century. They frequently exhibited at Exhibitions, and their stand in the Norwich Agricultural Hall may be remembered, small packets and samples being freely distributed to eager children clutching their paper carrier bags. In 1931 they purchased the old established grocery business of Thomas Bacon & Co. of Muspole Street, and formed a subsidiary company, Mancroft Food Products Limited, using the 'MANKROFT' trademark.

Mr. Henry John Copeman, Chairman and Governing Director, died on 21st July 1938, having been an active member of the company for 64 years. W.O.Copeman took over Henry's duties, and in 1943 the Board was further strengthened by the appointment of Harry William Englebright who had been employed as a clerk, traveller and buyer, for many years.

The premises in Castle Street and Davey Place were no longer adequate for the expanding business. Premises were purchased in Duke Street and extensive alterations were carried out, giving warehouse, garage and office space, the move being completed in July 1939, just six weeks before the the Second World War began. The main warehouse building comprised a ground floor area of 14,000 sq.ft., and there were first and second floors each of 10,000 sq.ft., together with docking bays, and an electric lift and conveyors to take goods to upper floors. Separate rooms were provided for the blending of tea, coffee roasting and grinding, the manufacture of baking powder, and the pre-packing of other commodities. Cold storage facilities were installed, and a special bacon room with ham cooking equipment adjoined the main ground floor of the warehouse. The garage, entered from Colegate, was large enough to house all the company's lorries and cars, and had workshop facilities.

The war brought an immediate escalation of demand for commodities of every description, and Copemans had to contend with permits, allocations, rations, not to mention endless Government forms! The number of rules and regulations ran into thousands. Part of their premises was taken over by the Ministry of Food, and housed hundreds of tons of essential foods in connection with the Ministry's scheme for dispersal of stocks. Mr. W.O. Copeman was appointed Chairman of the Eastern Area

A corner of the Sales Room in Duke Street.

Provisions and Groceries Advisory Committee to the Ministry of Food. In recognition of this work he received the O.B.E. in 1943.

They were very fortunate to escape with limited damage during the war years. During the Norwich 'blitz' surrounding buildings were engulfed in flames; Harmers in St. Andrews, St. Mary's Chapel, and many other properties nearby were either totally destroyed or badly damaged. Copemans were fortunate, and although a dozen or so incendiary bombs fell on the Duke Street premises, the prompt actions of their fire guards, and other members of staff, soon extinguished the

food rationing. He was impressed with the voluntary group system and in 1954 Copemans were among the first British wholesalers to form such a group with a relatively small number of retail grocers throughout East Anglia. MACE Marketing Services Ltd were launched in East Anglia by Copemans in 1960, and as the wholesale membership expanded to cover most of the United Kingdom and nearly 5000 affiliated retailers, it became the largest group of its kind in the country.

Steadily increasing trade made a move to new premises almost inevitable, and in the Spring of 1964 building was commenced on new purpose

The Duke Street premises.

flames without outside assistance, so that the damage, mainly to office machinery, was confined to a single room. The call-up of men into the Armed Forces also caused staffing problems, and during the course of the War 40 men and women joined various branches of the services. Fortunately all but one survived

After the war rationing still continued, and brought consequent problems, but conditions slowly returned to normal, and as more and more goods became available Copemans were again able to supply the retailers with a wider range of merchandise. In 1948 Mr. W.O. Copeman visited Canada and the United States to study developments in those countries which had not been affected by

built premises on a 3 acre site facing Drayton Road. It provided 36,000 sq.ft. of floor space on one level with a special asphalt finish designed to exploit the use of the fork lift truck. Adjoining the warehouse a secondary block housed the 4000 sq.ft. provisions department, with its specially constructed rooms for handling bacon and cheese, two bacon smoking stoves and 9600 cubic feet of refrigerated store. The offices were approached through the Main Entrance from Drayton Road. The Reception Area flanked by showrooms and a printing department, gave access to the principal offices, the staff canteen and welfare rooms. A smaller block providing garage and workshop space was entered from the main vehicle court.

JOHN COPEMAN & SONS LTD.

In 1966 Grimwade Ridley & Co. (Ipswich) Limited joined with Copemans under a new parent company, Copeman Ridley Limited.

On 21st October, 1970, disaster struck – fire destroyed the warehouse and part of the office block. Copemans immediately rented a large hangar at Fifer's Lane, Norwich, and within three weeks were re-stocked with goods and continuing their business. It took just nine months to rebuild their new premises on the same site on an even bigger scale than previously. The pleasant red brick buildings are set well back from Drayton Road, flanked by trees and a grass verge, which in spring-time is a welcome sight with its 'host of golden daffodils'.

Drayton Road site, Spring 1985.

Mr. W.O. Copeman's son, Roger Barrington Copeman, took over as Chairman in 1972. His father died in 1974, ending a life of service to his City and his Company, respected by all who knew him.

In February, 1983, Mr. Donald Bunyan, Managing Director of Copeman Ridley retired, after more than 45 years' service with the Company. He became a director of John Copeman & Sons in October, 1950, Managing Director in 1961 and Managing Director of Copeman Ridley in 1966. He had been a director of Mace Marketing services since 1967 and Distributive Marketing services since 1966. Under his guidance the company undertook a considerable amount of pioneering, including the introduction of fruit and vegetables, wines and spirits, frozen foods and fresh foods. Mr. Roger Copeman then became Chief Executive as well as Chairman.

On 23rd October 1987 the Copeman/Ridley organisation was purchased by Booker plc. who continue trading on the same site, and look forward to further extensions and expansion. They do not intend to retain the Copeman name and therefore, sadly, the family name that has been known and respected throughout the trading circles of the city and county for nearly two centuries will disappear from the building.

BULLARD & SONS, Ltd.,

BREWERS,

 NORWICH.

BULLARD & SONS LIMITED

Richard Bullard was born in the parish of St. John Maddermarket on 8th February, 1808. In 1828 at the church of St. John de Sepulchre he married Jane Yallop, who had been born in St. Peter Hungate on 20th March, 1811. They went to live at the top end of Oak Street, in St. Martin's, and as shown by an entry in the Vestry Book on 13th September, 1831, he was Overseer of the Parish. Later, with his wife and three children, Emma, Rachel and Ellen, he moved from there to the Excise Coffee House, Lower Goat Lane. In 1837, the first year of Queen Victoria's reign, he moved again, this time to premises near St. Miles' Bridge, which had been used as a dye office. There, in partnership with James Watts, he founded The Anchor Brewery.

Mr. Watts, a manufacturer, appears to have quickly lost interest in the brewing business, and the partnership was dissolved on 24th June 1847. Brewers were numerous in those days, and business correspondingly limited. There are, for instance, seventeen city brewers listed in White's Directory of 1854. But Richard Bullard was a shrewd man, and soon adopted a system of brewing that enabled him to supply beer that was extremely popular throughout the county. Business increased at such an extraordinary rate that more extensive buildings became necessary, surrounding properties were purchased, and new premises erected. These were opened in 1850, taking in a four acre site.

By 1853 he had ten children, including one set of twins, and had moved house to Poringland. He moved twice more, ending his days at Earlham, where he died on 3rd February 1864, aged 56. His obituary in the local paper said '. . . *The deceased, well known as a brewer and merchant, of extensive business, sprang from very humble life. By industry and constant application, he made the best use of the good intellect he was gifted with, and steadily raised himself to a foremost position amongst the traders of his city. Had he possessed the advantages of a good education, his name would have been more prominent in city affairs, but the sense of his deficiency in this respect kept him back. It was a distinguishing characteristic of the deceased that his great success, which has been rarely paralleled in our time, did not make him pretentious or purse proud, but was ever associated with singular modesty and unassuming manners. We allude to this especially, that young men may know that it is possible for energy, industry, and business talent to force their way even now-a-days through the greatest obstacles . . .*'

Harry Bullard, his fifth child, was born at the brewery site on 3rd March, 1841. He attended school at the Greyfriars Priory, Norwich, kept by Mr. William Brooks and later at a school in Church Street, East Dereham. Harry was not particularly studious, but was a keen and competent sportsman, and well liked by his contemporaries. On leaving school he went to London and worked for the firm of J. K. Hooper & Sons, Wine Merchants, Queenhithe. Subsequently, he visited vineyards in Spain and Portugal, travelling over the greater part of the terrain on horseback, and learned the art of making and blending fine wines.

On his return to Norwich Harry entered the family business. When Richard Bullard died in 1864 he was one of the Executors, the others being John Briggs, John Boyce (his sister Emma's husband), and his brother Charley. Three years later he married Miss Sarah Jane Ringer of Rougham.

Mr. Briggs died in 1874, when a Deed of Partnership was signed by Harry, Charley and Fred Bullard. and on the death of Charley, John Boyce became a Trustee partner with Harry and Fred.

Harry and Sarah Bullard had their first child, Mabel, who was born at East Carleton on 5th March, 1868. Others quickly followed – Herbert Harry was born 1869, Eva Mary in 1871, and Percy Ringer in 1872, all at Carleton Lodge. They later moved to Hellesdon House, where a further three children were born. Edward John in 1875, Gerald Thomas in 1875, Hilda May in 1879 and Freddy Ringer in 1882.

Harry Bullard Esq. Sheriff 1877 – 78, Mayor 1878 – 79 and 1879 – 80.

At the same time Harry's political career was prospering. In 1877 he was elected Sheriff of Norwich and in 1878 and 1879 he held the office of Mayor. However, 1878 was to be remembered as the year of the great flood. This began on the 16th November, just as darkness was setting in, the waters of the Wensum above New Mills, having over-flowed their banks, began to spread with startling rapidity upon the public road known as The Causeway at Heigham, and to penetrate up the connecting streets. Through Norwich itself the Wensum dashed madly along, to the amazement of the citizens, who saw its level gradually rising till warehouses and dwellings situated along its bank were inundated. A continuous rainfall added to the misery of the scene. Before ten o'clock on that Saturday evening parts of North Heigham, St. Michael Coslany, St. Lawrence, St. Swithin, St. Margaret and St. Mary were under water. Among the inhabitants of North Heigham in whose houses the water was gradually rising the greatest fear prevailed; and while hundreds fled from houses which were threatened, great numbers remained as occupants of upper rooms in the hope that in a few hours the water would subside.

The stout walls of the Anchor Brewery, situated near the river, received the full shock of the mighty torrent as it was whirled from the New Mills, and into its windows and doors which were constructed above what might fairly be supposed to be high water level, the waters poured for hours, until offices, stores and yards were inundated. At first, hopes were entertained that during the night the waters would abate; on the contrary with the increasing rainfall there had been a continuous rise, so that when morning dawned the area under water had been vastly extended and the position of many occupants of houses in the lowest lying districts, where the flood was deepest, was a matter of great concern. The next morning the Mayor, Sheriff and other civic dignitaries rode from district to district seeing what was required for the many hundreds of people who were rendered homeless and had no means of procuring food; they requisitioned boats of all kinds to rescue people, waggons and carts were sent down streets as far as they could go to rescue people from the upper windows, or to take provisions to those who preferred to stay prisoners in their own dwellings. Coffee, tea and bread were provided at distribution centres, and those whose houses had become untenable were given shelter in school-rooms. That Sunday evening there was a meeting in the Council Chamber. The city was in partial darkness as the floods had affected the Gas Works, and continuous rainfall all day meant that the waters were still rising. The Mayor exerted a calming influence on the Council and the citizens of Norwich. His expert organising ability meant that people and services were utilised to the best advantage, and for many years after that terrible flood people spoke of the way that Harry Bullard had served his City and its people during those desperate days.

The Anchor Brewery established a band in 1885, and Mr. E. J. Gaul was appointed band-master. That same year Harry Bullard was elected to represent his city in Parliament but was disqualified on petition on account of his agent's bribery. The citizens were so incensed by the decision that they paid his court costs. He served as Mayor again in 1886 and was Knighted by Queen Victoria. He was returned to Parliament with Samuel Hoare in 1890 and 1895, and in that year the firm was registered as Bullard & Sons Ltd, the three directors being Sir Harry Bullard (Chairman), Mr. John Boyce and Mr. George Arthur Coller. (A member of the firm of Coller & Son, coal merchants).

By the end of the 19th century the Anchor Brewery occupied substantial red brick buildings

second and sometimes a third mash took place. From the underback the wort was transferred to the three boiling coppers, capable of boiling five hundred barrels. The boiling was effected by steam brought from boilers below, and as soon as the boiling of the wort had commenced the hops were added, the duration of the boiling process varying according to the kind of beer being produced. The wort was next run off into a series of vessels known as 'hop-backs', (where the wort was strained and the hops kept back). On the top floor of the brewery were the coolers, which had a capacity of upwards

Fermenting vats at Bullard's Brewery.

covering an area of about seven acres. There were well appointed offices and sample rooms. In the brewery upstairs the mashing house contained two huge tuns capable together of mashing one hundred and fifty-five quarters. The malt was hoisted in sacks to the mash-house from a platform below. It was then shot through hoppers into roller mills, where it was crushed, having been previously screened and separated. It was next conveyed by what was known as a 'Jacob's ladder' to a hopper, and then to one of Steel's patent machines, in which it became macerated with water, before being passed to the mash-tub. In the mash-tub it was further amalgamated with water by means of a series of revolving rakes. When this process was sufficiently advanced the infusion or 'wort' was passed through a strainer to the 'underback', and a

of six hundred barrels a day. Three Morton refrigerators were employed in effecting the cooling, which was further assisted by the free admission of air. In an adjacent portion of the building were the eighteen fermenting tuns, capable of holding about one hundred and fifty barrels each. Here the yeast was added and fermentation took place. After the lapse of from four to seven days fermentation was complete, the yeast was removed, and the beer ran in pipes to the racking rooms, where it was put into barrels for storage or despatch.

Norwich beer, famed for its flavour, owed much to the quality of the water. In the Anchor Brewery this was drawn from an artesian well dug deeply in the chalk under the brewery. This was pumped to water cisterns at the top of the brewery which had an aggregate capacity of fifteen thousand gallons.

BULLARD & SONS LTD.

Huge cellars were also dug out of the chalk for use as stores, capable of accommodating six thousand barrels. In the two racking rooms, which could deal with one thousand five hundred barrels, the beer was run into casks. One of these rooms communicated by means of an hydraulic lift, with the scalding yard, where by the combined action of steam and hot water the possibility of tainted casks was removed. The steam was supplied from four boilers, one of 60 h.p. and three of 40 h.p.

Cleaning the barrels at Bullard's Brewery.

Bullards had their own fitting, turning, smiths', shoeing and wheelwrights' shops, so that they not only made their own casks and carts, but shoed their own horses and effected their own repairs of machinery. The stables contained stall and loose-box accommodation for one hundred horses. There were coach-houses and harness room, painters' and joiners' shops and a well stocked timber yard. In common with so many other businesses in Norwich at this time, they were indeed very self-sufficient.

The malthouses were separate from the brewery, some being located in other parts of the city and county. There were three malting floors in the brewery, and the malt produced was mainly made from Norfolk barley. Germination generally took about twelve to fourteen days to complete.

The range of Bullards' products was extensive. They produced Light Pale Ale, East India Pale Ale, Imperial Ale, and other strong ales, London Stout, and a double stout 'of a nourishing character'. The firm also produced wines and spirits, being importers as well as merchants, and held large stocks in bond at Yarmouth and Norwich.

Yet the time was one of cut-throat competition for brewers, and it is easy to see why so many of the small brewers went out of business. The sheer size of brewing operations in terms of labour, machinery, buildings and materials meant it was too costly for all but the large, well established companies to survive.

Fortunately, Bullards had their business well in order when John Boyce died in 1900, aged 69. Donald Gaul, who had been Company Secretary

since its inception, was appointed to the vacant seat on the Board. Subsequently, Sir Harry Bullard died in December, 1903 and his son Edward John was also appointed to the Directorate. Mr. Ernest Bullard, Charley's son, also joined the business, and Sir Harry's son, Gerald Thomas, had control of the Mineral Water Manufactory, which had been opened in Lower Westwick Street in 1897, and unusually included cloakrooms and breakfast rooms for the workers.

Bullards continued to expand and prosper, becoming one of the four great brewery companies of Norwich. By 1937 Mr. Gerald Bullard, a fourth generation descendant of the founder had joined the firm. He had attended the Birmingham School of Brewing after leaving Cambridge, and started as a shift brewer, working long hours at times between 4 a.m. and 6 p.m.

In 1942, during the Second World War, the maltings on St. Swithin's Terrace were bombed, but despite the damage they were patched up and carried on working.

By 1950 Mr. Gerald Bullard, having served in the Royal Navy, returned to the family firm, and joined the Board, becoming Chairman the following year. Mr. Bullard said he thought the reason so many local brewers had gone out of business was due to the enormous increase in the value of their properties. The great difficulty for any brewing company was to ensure an adequate return on the capital assets, and this applied particularly to the smaller breweries.

Bullard's chimney in the 1940's.

In 1957 Bullards enlarged their brewing capacity, and erected an extension to their bottling store. Then, a year later they bought up Youngs,

Crawshay & Youngs' brewery in King Street. Finally, in 1961, John Morse, Chairman of Steward & Patteson, and Gerald Bullard joined their resources and bought Morgans. As Gerald Bullard said: 'We were, of course, largely interested in the properties. There were about 400 of them, mainly in Norfolk and Norwich, and they were shared out one morning between us – we cut cards to see who should have first pick'. Mr. Bullard also said that both brewery companies were interested in the properties as licensed houses, and fully intended to keep most of them open. They foresaw that some rationalisation would be necessary, but this was not the main purpose of the acquisition. Bullards at that time owned over 1,000 public houses. In the same year they sold off Morgan's brewery in King Street to Watneys, who wanted a brewery to supply their free trade outlets in the area.

Despite their growth, the firm could not compete against the big national brewers, several of whom were angling for a take-over. In 1963 Mr. Bullard was told by Simon Combe, Chairman of Watneys, that they were buying shares of Bullards and Steward & Patteson in the open market. When they had purchased about 18% of each company, Gerald Bullard told Simon Combe that Watneys must make a proper bid, or the fact that they were making purchases of shares would have to be disclosed to the shareholders. The bid was then negotiated and accepted on behalf of the shareholders, so that the two public companies passed to Watneys, and John Morse and Gerald Bullard joined the board of Watney Mann Limited, in London.

The *Eastern Evening News* of 18th October, 1966, announced that brewing was to stop at the Anchor Brewery. Instead Bullards' beers would be produced at the Watney Mann brewery at King Street, and taken by road tanker to the Anchor site for racking, bottling and despatch.

Five years later the 3 acre site of the old Anchor Brewery was offered for sale by Watney Mann. The buildings on the site had already been stripped of all their brewing equipment and fittings. The property was purchased by Mr. R. G. Lawrence of Colney Hall in July 1972, and from then on the buildings on the site were left derelict; they were vandalised, stripped of materials by a group of demolition men, and although the old fermenting plant was a listed building, the whole complex was neglected and, by 1975, in a steadily worsening state of repair.

Eventually the Norwich City Council agreed a scheme of redevelopment for the area, and today we have a pleasant and attractive complex of houses and flats, which has brought people back to live in the City centre. I think it is sad, however, that they demolished the brewery chimney, a familiar and well-loved landmark to so many Norwich people.

Bullard's Brewery site 1988 – an attractive housing complex.

At the end of October, 1974, Gerald Bullard retired as Chairman of Watney Mann (East Anglia) Limited and so ended a family association with brewing in Norwich, which began 137 years earlier when Richard Bullard took over the premises later known as The Anchor Brewery.

Famous sign used by Bullards, painted by Sir Arthur Munnings.

BONDS (NORWICH) LTD

Bonds of Norwich has been well-known throughout the county for over 100 years, and has supplied generations of Norfolk families with quality merchandise.

Like so many aspects of Norwich trade and manufacture, the magnificent store in All Saints Green had its beginnings towards the end of the 19th century. It was founded by Robert Herne Bond, a farmer's son, born in Ludham in 1844, who in 1879 came to Norwich with his wife Mary Anne. He bought a small drapery shop at No. 19 Ber Street belonging to a Mr. Woodland. At first they lived over the shop and there Mrs. Bond looked after her family and found time to make hats for the business. She also looked after members of staff who 'lived in'.

The extent of his property buying is outlined by Kelly's Directory of 1896, where he is listed as a general draper at Nos.19 and 21 Ber Street. and at Nos. 62 & 64 Bridge Street, St. George's (on the west side between Blackfriar's Bridge and Colegate). One year later his oldest son, William, joined the business.

The keynote of the business at this time was familial sufficiency. John Bond, the second son, became an architect, and it was he, as the business continued to expand, who designed the many extensions carried out on the original store, which in the early days only fronted Ber Street. His firm, of J. Owen Bond, continued later by his son Robert, was responsible for development within the store until the end of the 1970s.

The first shop in Ber Street.

They had six children, William, Jessie, John, Ida, Eva (known as Gussie), and Ernest, three of whom were born prior to the move to Ber Street.By 1886 Robert had prospered sufficiently to purchase three adjoining properties, including the Jubilee public house, kept by victualler Edward Wilson.

Early trading records are not available but it is said that a glass of sherry or port, or a quarter pound of tea, provided inducement to customers spending the princely sum of a golden sovereign

Ernest Charles Bond was educated at The Commercial School, St. Andrews. He left Norwich in 1895 and worked in the drapery trade in other towns, before joining the family business in 1903. He served in the 2A Battery, H.A.C. during the First World War, during which time his sister Ida served in the shop.

The Arcade.

It was at this time that Bonds began to take on a more recognisably modern air. In 1914 the Arcade on All Saints Green was opened, thus giving the business frontages on two wide streets. Similarly, Robert's wife, Mary Anne Bond laid the foundations of the millinery department, which was to become one of the biggest outside the West End of London. By the late 1930s more than 30 assistants were selling hats, and more than 20 milliners were employed making them. The busy day in the week was Saturday, when more than 1,000 hats would be sold, mainly priced between 3s.11d. and 9s.11d. (20p. and 50p). To cope with the demand the buyer had to go to London at least once, and sometimes twice a week, to obtain fresh supplies.

Robert Herne Bond died in 1924. The business continued under William and Ernest, with William (who died in 1944) becoming Chairman. They attracted more and more 'county trade', that vital requisite for the early shopkeeper, selling, amongst other things, servants' uniforms, frocks and aprons.

Further growth came when the lease of the Thatched Cinema expired in April, 1930 and the property was taken over by Bonds for use as Restaurant, Conference Hall and Ballroom. Mr. Richard Bond recalls the sprung floor, suspended all the way round on chains, which literally 'bounced' when walked upon. When used as a cinema a false sloping floor had been laid on top. It was later used as a display window and store, but private functions were often held in evenings and dances took place on Saturday nights, when the room had to be cleared. Dinners were often held for 300 to 400 people, when special gas stoves were wheeled into the corridor running beside the Ballroom. Presumably it was because of owning the Thatched Ballroom that the firm's sports club at Trowse was called 'The Tudor Athletic Club'.

Bonds operated a strict training policy. It was the custom for staff to serve a three year apprenticeship, and in most cases pay for the privilege, but Ernest was against this, so apprentices were paid 6s. per week plus lunches. Their first year was spent packing, and unpacking, disentangling string, smoothing out tissue paper, picking up pins, and brushing and dusting the vast departmental displays. After three years they were promoted to 'improvers' and were then occasionally allowed to serve if all the sales staff were busy. All fashion garments carried a 'Bonds' label which had to be sewn in, and this was one of the 'improvers' jobs, as

The Millinery Department.

well as going through all stock to ensure that buttons were secure!

Staff worked on commission and the showroom girls thought themselves somewhat superior – they wore long green dresses and black shoes, often made of satin at 1s.11d. per pair. When these became shabby they were painted over with black ink. They worked from 9 a.m. to 6 p.m. and 8 p.m. on Fridays and Saturdays. At Christmas Ernest would give the apprentices and 'improvers' 10s.

Eric John Sidney Hinde married Marjorie, only daughter of Ernest Bond, in 1931, and joined the firm, having spent five years working on the London Stock Exchange. Educated at the Norwich School, Gresham's School and Corpus Christi College, Cambridge, he had graduated in Economics and Law.

Ida Bond became a Non-Executive Director in

1936, and Ernest's son Richard joined the firm in 1937. Bonds prided themselves on the fact that they could provide a family's needs from the cradle to the grave and used the slogan 'Bonds Goods are Good Goods'.

By 1939 the store had become a large organisation, employing over 200 people. But war clouds were gathering. Eric Hinde was commissioned in the R.A.S.C. and was a prisoner-of-war Singapore from 1942-1945, and Richard Bond served in the R.A.(A.A.) 1939-1946 with the rank of Captain. Bonds suffered badly from the air raids of 1942. When the bombs fell, despite heroic attempts by firemen, flames engulfed the timber framework, and a massive blaze ripped through the whole building. The whole premises were completely destroyed including the delightful Thatched Ballroom.

In common with so many other old established Norwich businesses, Ernest Bond did not allow the war damage to stop their trading. Within three days they were selling what was left of the stock from buses they had bought and placed on their bomb-ravaged car park. The restaurant continued in business from a tin shed, also in the car park, and was later transferred to St. Catherine's House, now the home of the British Broadcasting Corporation in Norwich. Other departments moved into the building now occupied by Barclays Bank in Orford Place, and the furniture and carpet departments were moved into two large semi-detached premises on Thorpe Road, later occupied by Tibbenham Advertising Limited.

In Kelly's Directory of 1933 Bonds still only occupy Nos. 9 to 23, and The Arcade, All Saints

Bonds pre-war.

BONDS (NORWICH) LTD.

Green, but in the great re-building programme completed in 1951, the whole shape and style of this part of Ber Street and All Saints Green changed. A

THE NEW FUR FABRIC

Makes the Ideal Occasional

COATS

✳

FOR MORNING AFTERNOON and EVENING WEAR

✳

Inexpensive and Indistinguishable from Fur; there is a style and shade for every occasion at

BONDS

Where the most Moderate Purse will buy the Smartest Fashions ! !

Swagger Style Mole Marking, Fur Fabric For morning or over an evening frock. In Nigger, Beige, Fawn and Grey. Sizes 8, 9, W & WX.

45/-

Also Nigger and Black in Lamb Marking at **40/-**

Definitely Smart !
The new short Fur Fabric Coat in shades of Black, Nigger, lined Silk to tone. Sizes 8, 9, S.W. **37/6**

BONDS of NORWICH
ALL SAINTS GREEN & BER STREET

great new, modern, department store arose from the ashes with the emphasis on quality and personal service, which had enhanced their former reputation. In 1960 when the well-known firm of Greens of the Haymarket closed down, Bonds acquired the stock and goodwill, and in 1962 they opened a branch in East Dereham, taking over and modernising Clutten's.

Eric Hinde played his part in the civic life of the city. He returned to the Council in 1947, and was elected Lord Mayor in 1951. He became an Alderman in 1955, and a Magistrate in 1960. His son Nicholas joined the business in 1957, and was made a Director in 1961, when his father became

After the Blitz – 1942.

Serving customers from buses in the car park the morning after the air raids.

Managing Director. Ernest remained as Chairman, with Richard as Vice-Chairman, a real family business.

Bonds centenary was celebrated with much pomp in 1979. An *Eastern Evening News* Advertiser's Supplement of 26th March, 1979, remarked *'It is stepping into its second century with an updated, modernised and expanded image. For last year £1 million was spent on the biggest re-development since the war, adding 14,000 sq.ft. of selling space, making in all 96,000 sq.ft. with many new features. It now has an attractive and individual first floor rustic restaurant which seats 160, a new two-storey extension housing a large confectionery and stationery department and a flower shop, a wine cellar in the basement, and a second floor hairdressing and beauty salon. The store has been re-organised with escalators, automatic doors and a more spacious lay-out, and ground and first floor have been re-carpeted.'*

The Centenary was launched with a dinner for Bond's 400 members of staff and guests at St. Andrew's Hall. Six great-great-grandchildren of Mr. Robert Herne Bond were at the dinner.

Yet commercial pressures were gathering. Mr. Hinde remarked *'It is increasingly difficult to run a private store, so it is a big challenge to keep the shop going as part of the family'*. All the Directors, except one, were members of the Bond family. The board, then in its fourth generation, included the Chairman, Mr. Richard Bond, the founder's great-grandsons Mr. Nicholas and Mr. Stephen Hinde, and great-granddaughter, Miss Susan Bond.

Subsequently, as if in testimony to those remarks, Bonds was purchased by the John Lewis Partnership, who are building a giant extension and multi-storey car park, and will then become the largest store in Norwich. They have retained the name BONDS, and will continue to provide their customers with the quality merchandise and efficient service that the people of the city and county have received from this great store for more than a century.

BOULTON & PAUL

BOULTON & PAUL LIMITED

In 1797 William Moore, aged 33, of Warham, came to Norwich, and opened an Ironmonger's shop in Cockey Lane. A few years later he took into partnership John Hilling Barnard, and the name of the firm became Moore & Barnard, ironmongers and stove grate manufacturers. Their shop lay on the corner of Little London Street, facing London Street, later the site of Garlands' store.

William Moore took an active part in civic affairs and received the Freedom of the City on 24th February 1807. He was Sheriff in 1823, elected alderman for St. Stephen's ward on 12th April 1833, and became Mayor in 1835. He was sworn in on 16th June 1835, and this was the occasion of the last Guild Day held in Norwich before much of the civic splendour was swept away under the terms of the Municipal Reform Act. That evening he dined 800 guests in St. Andrew's Hall

When Moore died in 1839 John Hilling Barnard took into partnership his brother Dennis, but he soon retired. William Staples Boulton then joined him as a partner and the firm became Barnard & Boulton.

By 1850 they had moved to the other side of London Street and in 1853 took as an apprentice a 12 year old boy by the name of J. J. Dawson Paul. John Hilling Barnard died in 1862 at his house on All Saints Green and on 1st January 1863 Mr. Boulton advertised in the newspaper that the firm would, in future, be carried on in his name only.

In 1865 a small factory was opened in Rose Lane and Dawson Paul was made Manager at a salary of £100 per year, with a house rent and rates free in the factory grounds. The property had been leased by George Jay from the Girls' Hospital Trustees, Ladyday 1853, and was transferred to Boulton in

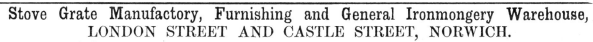

Stove Grate Manufactory, Furnishing and General Ironmongery Warehouse, LONDON STREET AND CASTLE STREET, NORWICH.

Gentlemen building or furnishing are respectfully invited to inspect **Barnard & Boulton's** Stock of Dining and Drawing Room Stoves, and Bedroom Registers, with or without Fire-Brick Backs ; Air Stoves ; Cookeries, with open or close Fires ; Hot Plates, Smoke Jacks, &c. Their Furnishing Stock consists of Fenders and Fireirons in every variety ; Paper and Japanned Trays, Urns, best Sheffield and London Cutlery, Plated Goods, Lamps of every kind, Baths, Tin, Copper, and Britannia Metal Goods, Water Filters, **Iron Bedsteads** and **Cribs,** and every Article connected with this branch of the business. They have arranged the General Ironmongery towards *Castle Street,* as well as Colors and Oils, Traces, Backbands, Chains, Pigs' Troughs, Eaves Spouting and Rain Pipe, Weighing Machines, Painters' Brushes, &c. ; also, a large assortment of Fishing Tackle and Rods, Guns, Powder and Shot, Flasks, Pouches and Belts, Dram Bottles, &c.
Iron Hurdles, wrought and cast-iron Palisading and Gates, and Iron Work of every description. Strained Wire Fencing. Wire Game and Sheep Netting.
Greenhouses and Pits heated with Hot Water on simple and approved principles. Bell Hanging and Smiths' Work in general.
B. & B. are always happy to give estimates for the supply of New Houses with every requisite in their way, including Bricklayers' Work, &c.

Barnard and Boulton shop front — 1850's.

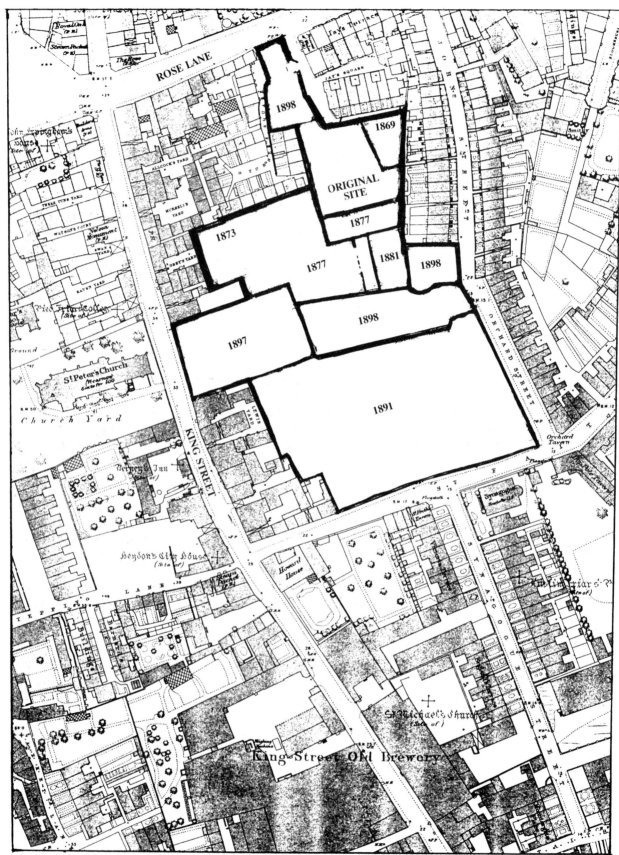

Ordnance survey map 1885 — marked to show how Boulton & Paul took over the site between Rose Lane, King Street and Mountergate.

1864. Three years later he sold the ironmongery business to Messrs. Piper & Theobald (later Johnson, Burton & Theobald), and devoted all his energies to the manufacturing part of the concern in Rose Lane.

Bayne 1869 gives a description of the works: '*Mr. W. S. Boulton, who occupies extensive premises in Rose Lane, is a manufacturer of agricultural and horticultural implements; also of strained wire fencing, iron hurdles, park gates, garden chairs, iron bedsteads, kitchen ranges, hot-water apparatus, etc. He produces every kind of railing, and palisading round Chapel Field, which is a great ornament as well as protection to the ground. He also supplies a great variety of useful machines, such as mincing and sausage machines, and almost all articles made of iron.*'

Boulton continued buying up property – one site included Watt's foundry where the old prison treadmill had been built. He had married a local girl, Elizabeth Duffield in 1868, and they lived near the Rose Lane factory, where, it is said he rang a loud bell every morning at 6 a.m. to call the men to work.

1868 saw an important technological innovation with the installation of wire netting machines. They started with three machines producing 2ft, 3ft and 4ft wide netting respectively. The looms were constructed almost entirely of wood and were extremely difficult to use. They had to work day and night in order to keep up with the demand. A year later Mr. Paul was taken into partnership and the firm became Boulton & Paul.

Natural and unnatural disasters preyed on the businesses of 19th century Norwich. Boulton & Paul's misfortune was a disastrous fire in August 1876 which started in the carpenters' shop. Though Colmans sent their Fire Brigade to help, it still destroyed the carpenters' shop and other parts of the works. Boulton & Paul were insured against loss of plant and building but not for the consequential loss of business. The firm pulled through but Mr. Boulton never really recovered from the blow. He suffered badly from rheumatism and rarely left his house, leaving the running of the company to the younger man, and dying finally in 1879. Dawson Paul was left with the huge task of running a business which employed 350 men, making a profit, and paying off Mrs. Boulton for her share under the terms of his agreement with Boulton. Fortunately he had, by this time, obtained the confidence of his bankers, and with their help he prospered, making many changes and additions, and putting down a galvanizing plant.

It is at this point that another Barnard enters the story. John Neville Barnard, son of a builder and not related to the family of the firm, had received his training at Howes & Son, engineers. He then joined the firm of Smithdale & Sons, engineers, who were the builders of the new engines employed for

driving the machinery for the extension of Boulton & Paul's works, and which were fixed under his supervision in 1882. On completion of the work Mr. Barnard took on the superintendence of the engineering department at the Rose Lane Works.

At this time the works were rapidly developing, especially in the wire netting department, and Mr. Barnard designed and built fast running and more efficient wire netting machinery.

Mr. Dawson Paul was Sheriff of Norwich in 1885, and in December of that year he and his wife entertained the employees and their wives to dinner in St. Andrew's Hall. One feature of the evening was the first public appearance of the Rose Lane Works Band.

On 10th May 1890 another serious fire occurred, this time at the wharf, damage being estimated at between £4,000 and £5,000.

Boulton & Paul became a Limited Company on 14th December 1897, with J.J. Dawson Paul as Governing Director and Henry ffiske, who had been made a partner four years previously, Managing Director. The same year even more property was purchased in King Street and a smithy and fencing shops were erected. Whilst pulling down some cottages on the site it was discovered they had once been part of a city merchant's great hall. The timbers were used in the construction of their new offices in Rose Lane in 1899, a building we all know as The Tudor Hall. In another house a fine moulded ceiling was discovered and this was dismantled and placed in Mr. Paul's office. At an entrance to one of the passages leading to William Street was a carved Elizabethan door frame: if you walk down the side of Tudor Hall you will see it is still preserved in the east wall of the building.

Joseph John Dawson Paul, crowned his civic achievements by becoming Mayor in 1900, and it fell to him to proclaim the accession of King Edward VII in Norwich Market Place. He was Deputy Lieutenant of Norfolk in 1906, a Director of the Norwich Union Life Office, a Trustee of The Bethel Hospital, and held many other offices and appointments. He had a son, Captain J. Dawson Paul, and three daughters.

By this time the firm had expanded its range of products and were well-known for the production of a wide variety of goods, including glasshouses, orangeries, vineries and palm-houses, which were exported all over the world. This was the age of the 'conservatory' and many of them cost thousands of pounds. They supplied 1,500 ft. of piping for the Plantation Garden in Norwich, and supplied both boiler and conservatory. Aviaries were made for Somerleyton Hall, and 'convenient' suburban residences were made in galvanised iron, together with fishing 'temples', boat-houses, portable iron studios and ornamental bridges.

Unbeknown to their fathers, it is said, young Dawson Paul and Geoffrey ffiske, designed a highly

BOULTON & PAUL, ROSE LANE WORKS, NORWICH.

JOINERS SHOP

REBUILT 1876

BOULTON, PAUL SC

FLOOR AREA OF GREENHOUSE BUILDING DEPARTMENT 40,000 FEET.

successful boat called the 'Dollydo', and fitted it out with one of the firm's marine engines. They were so successful in their first race that everyone else withdrew from racing for the remainder of the season. Thereafter the firm did make a few motorboats, and a couple of twenty-one foot international class motor boats, the *'Fuji-Yama'* and the *'Vicuna'*.

Advertisement – early 1900's.

In 1910 they built the sledges for Robert Falcon Scott's ill-fated expedition to the Antarctic.

The First World War, which began with the cancellation of orders, and the speedy return home of employees who were abroad, soon provided opportunities when the the turmoil subsided, and Boulton & Paul became extremely busy fulfilling many contracts which included a Naval Hospital at Dover, huts and stables for 6,000 men and horses which had to be completed in ten weeks, a prisoner-of-war camp in Jersey, hangars for the Royal Flying Corps, Naval and Military Installations, steel-framed buildings in arsenals and dockyards, hospitals in France and warehouses in Mesopotamia. The Fencing Department turned their attention to making field kitchens and drum barrows for telegraph wire, and the Engine Department made electric lighting plant for mobile workshops, portable pumps for trenches and marine engines.

But the most momentous news came in 1915, when they were asked to make aeroplanes. William ffiske took charge of the woodworking and commercial side of the project, whilst Stanley Howes (of Howes & Sons, Engineers – who had also wanted to help the war effort) agreed to undertake the erection and assembly of the aircraft. Eventually some 2,000 people were employed on this work at the Rose Lane Works.

They still needed somewhere for the final assembly and where the finished aircraft could take off, and eventually laid out an airfield on the old Cavalry Drill Ground on Mousehold. By October, 1915, the first aeroplane was completed and awaiting its test. Production continued and rapidly outgrew the Rose Lane Works. Consequently, it was decided to transfer to a 14 acre site on the other side of the river, which we all know as Riverside Works. The buildings were quickly erected and the transfer was made at Easter, 1916. They made 550 F.E.s, 1,550 Sopwith Camels, and later Snipe, a modification of the Camel. In all 2,530 military aircraft were completed.

In collaboration with other East Anglian firms they made shells, and a company, Norwich Components Limited was set up to manufacture fuses; it produced more than two million, and when the old warehouse in which it operated was burned to the ground in 1917, they took over the city's skating rink.

At the end of the war the two older men stood down and control was vested in a Committee of Management made up of Captain Paul, William ffiske, Stanley Howes and Geoffrey ffiske. It was decided to concentrate all their efforts on the Riverside site and the Rose Lane site was sold to the Co-operative Wholesale Society for use as a shoe factory.

The wood-working department was, however, the most important, and the post-war demand was for wooden buildings – sports pavilions, club-houses, parish halls, huts for holiday camps, poultry houses, etc. The first Club House for the Norwich Aero Club on Mousehold was a Boulton & Paul sectional building.

J.D.North, a young man already well-known as a designer in the aircraft industry, had joined the firm in 1917. He now felt the day of the wooden aircraft was over, and wanted to build in steel. The first metal aircraft was a light two-seater with a top speed of 104 m.p.h. It was the first all metal aeroplane to be made in Britain and was exhibited at the Paris Exhibition in November 1919. They made a standard twin-engined day bomber for the Royal Air Force called the Bolton, and others were called the Bodmin and the Bugle. They also built 70 flying boat hulls for the Navy, and 7,835 propellers. By

Making aeroplanes at Mousehold during the First World War. (Two of my aunts are in the photo).

Norwich guide 1936.

1926 North had designed the first example of a twin-engined, all metal biplane bomber named the Sidestrand, and this was taken into service by No.101 Squadron of the Royal Air Force. This aeroplane was later superseded by The Overstrand, the main improvement being a pneumatically operated gun turret fitted in the nose.

But a very exciting project was on the drawing board. The Government wanted airships, and with North acting as consultant, the R.101 was designed at the Royal Airship Works at Cardington. It was a task of immense technical difficulty. Construction was started at the Riverside Works. 27 miles of tubing, 11 miles of bracing cables, 65,000 nuts and bolts, made up the sections, all of which were manufactured at Norwich, and then sent to Cardington to be bolted together. So exact were the engineers measurements and the superb workmanship that not one piece had to be returned to Norwich for correction. And when that great airship was completed she flew over the city and all the population turned out to cheer and wave as she passed overhead. Sadly, on a stormy night in October, 1930, she crashed at Beauvais, on her way to India. There had been some misgivings about her colossal size, but it was officially stated at the enquiry that no responsibility for the loss lay in the design or manufacture of the hull.

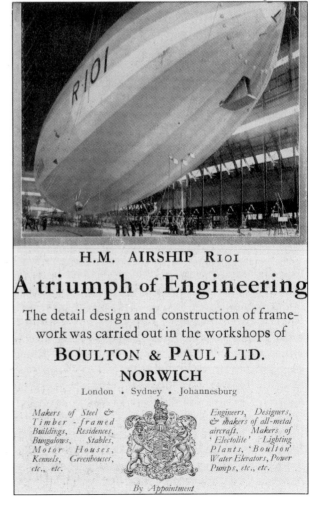

H.M. AIRSHIP R101

A triumph of Engineering

The detail design and construction of framework was carried out in the workshops of

BOULTON & PAUL LTD.
NORWICH

London • Sydney • Johannesburg

Makers of Steel & Timber-framed Buildings, Residences, Bungalows, Stables, Motor Houses, Kennels, Greenhouses, etc., etc.

Engineers, Designers, & makers of all-metal aircraft. Makers of 'Electolite' Lighting Plants, 'Boulton' Water Elevators, Power Pumps, etc., etc.

By Appointment

R101 moored at Cardington.

Just four years later Boulton & Paul sold the aircraft division to North and it moved to Wolverhampton, although retaining its name.

In 1935 Captain Paul left the organisation and Richard Jewson, a Norwich timber merchant, took over the Chairmanship of the Company. Mr. C.W. Hayward and Mr. Jean H. Tresfon also joined Geoffrey ffiske, Stanley Howes and Harry Towlson, (Company Secretary), on the Board of Directors.

Boulton & Paul continued to experiment and diversify; tea and coffee factories, a market in Manchester, the Gates at Gibraltar, Piers at Wallasey and New Brighton, and a hut for the Police outside Thorpe Station. Nothing too big, too small, or too difficult, was outside the scope of their ingenuity.

The constructional steel department was by now firmly established, having received an order in 1928 for pylons for the National Grid, taking up 25,000 tons of steel. They erected airport buildings, Dutch barns, theatres, cinemas, studios, and an ice-rink at Blackpool. They struggled through the depression of the 1930s, and became involved in the re-armament programme, making camps for the Forces, and a box shop was set up for making all manner of boxes for military purposes – one million were made by May 1940. Component parts were also made for the Airspeed Oxford Trainer.

The steel-working capacity was doubled in 1937 and the department became one of the best equipped in the country. This department grew steadily in importance under the direction of Richard Taylor

and was heavily involved in the 'shadow factory' building programme at the outbreak of the second world war. They made huge packing cases for bombs, later utilised as huts for airfield staff, the fuselage for Oxford trainers, noses for Horsa gliders, and wire netting track was laid over grass and sand to form runways. Factories and radio masts were constructed, 85,400 Morrison air-raid shelters, and frames for tank transporters (which featured on the beaches of Dunkirk). In total they produced something like 13 million pounds worth of goods during the war years. However, they did not escape unscathed. They were one of the firms earmarked for destruction by the German Air Force. Bombed on several occasions, many of their staff were killed or injured. Flames and destruction there may have been, but the employees carried on with their work, helped by A.R.P. and Fire Service personnel.

Subsidiary companies had been acquired and after the war contributed to the group's increased capacity. The Midland Woodworking Company at Melton Mowbray was the largest, and in 1946 Mr.A.F.Clarke, their Managing Director, joined the Board. Woodworking capabilities were increased, and the structural steel department had full order books. A clothing factory at Merton, a Hawker factory at Slough, eight hundred tons of steel for a sugar beet factory at Cantley, business was brisk, the employees worked hard, and the order books were full during the post-war boom years.

They made furniture for the Ministry of Supply, and a batch of pedaloes – the prototype was tested in the Wensum by two somewhat 'weighty' gentlemen, Dick Taylor, by now Managing Director, and George Fish, Manager of the Woodworking Department. One notable contract was the supply of base huts for the Trans-Antarctic Expedition – the leader, Vivian Fuchs, paid a number of visits to the Riverside Works.

DRAYTON WOOD, DRAYTON, NORFOLK.

Complete Heating carried out by
BOULTON & PAUL, LTD.

Alongside this, a limited amount of domestic joinery was produced, but overall very little profit was made. The Midland Woodworking Company, on the other hand, had reverted to standard joinery production and with the housing boom began to prosper.

In 1948 a South African Company, Anglo-Transvaal Industries Limited, bought 500,100 ordinary shares – the controlling interest – in Boulton & Paul from Mr. J.H.Tresfon, by then Managing Director. Mr. Tresfon said there would be no change in the management or the policy of Boulton & Paul or its subsidiaries. The Company's interests had expanded rapidly in South Africa with the development of the Union. Mr. Tresfon joined the board of Anglo-Transvaal and became its Chairman and M.D., whilst continuing as Chairman and M.D. of Boulton & Paul, Norwich.

Inevitably, in 1956, the Company made the decision to abandon all other forms of woodworking and concentrate on standard joinery, and eventually the sales organisation of the two companies (Norwich & Melton Mowbray) were merged.

But other forms of retrenchment were in hand. In 1957 it was announced that the sheet metal section, employing some 30 men, was to close. No further outside orders would be accepted. That same year an agreement was made that Boulton & Paul would take a financial interest in Anglian Building Products and its associated companies, Atlas Sand & Gravel, and Norwich Ready-Mixed Concrete, whose offices and works were at Lenwade. They specialised in reinforced and pre-cast concrete. Fortunately for Boulton & Paul they ended this association just prior to the Ronan Point disaster.

On 9th September 1959 they took over the old established business of C.Moreland, Hayne & Co. Ltd., constructional engineers, with works on the London docks, and in June, 1960, they also took over the Tusting Scaffolding Company. It was said the company would operate independently under its existing name at its address in Mile Cross Lane, and Mr. Osborne Tusting would remain Director, with Mr. R. Talbot, the Manager, also joining the board.

A major decision was made to set up a factory in Lowestoft, and in January, 1961, work started on a new joinery factory, costing £920,000, on a somewhat water-logged site at Lowestoft. This was opened in 1962 for the receipt of timber and the machining of components for assembly at Norwich and Melton Mowbray.

The business was at this time expanding so rapidly that within a year or so the capacity at Lowestoft was increased by one third, and before long was working both night and day to cope with the demand. Looking back, it is thought by some members of the Boulton & Paul staff that this could have been the beginning of the end for the Norwich woodworking department. What was the point of sending component parts a mere 26 miles to a

An aerial photograph of the Boulton & Paul works comprising structural engineering workshops, woodworking factory and wire working factory – 1935.

factory at Norwich, which was, in any event, badly placed for distribution purposes?

In the late 1960s the Essex Company of John Sadd was acquired, and flush door production was added to the range. John Sadd had a number of Builders' Merchants' outlets in Essex – these were to become the first of the current 50 or so Joinery Centres now spread around the Country for the sale of standard joinery. (The John Sadd Merchanting Division of Boulton & Paul were sold to Jewson & Sons, the Norwich based timber and builders' merchants subsidiary of the International Timber Corporation in December, 1978).

September, 1968 the *Eastern Daily Press* reported: *'It was announced yesterday that British Electric Traction now hold between 50%/51% of the issued voting capital of Boulton & Paul, one of the largest employers in the Norwich area, and thus controls the firm. The take-over is unlikely to affect the jobs of the 3,000 employees, more than half of them in the Norwich and Lowestoft works and subsidiaries.'* Subsequently press notices listed a catalogue of reductions:

1974: Two hundred workers made redundant, mostly in joinery shops, 60 in Lowestoft, 50 at Norwich, and others at Melton Mowbray and Maldon.

1976: A subsidiary company of Boulton & Paul making aluminium windows at Eversley Road, Norwich, closes down with loss of 250 jobs.

1980: Mr. Ray Chenhall, Group Managing Director, announces that half the joinery assembly depot was to be made redundant, due to poor demand for joinery products.

1981: More than 300 workers became redundant because of a fall in orders for structural steelwork. They included manual workers, clerical, technical and managerial posts.

1982: Fifty more jobs were lost in steel fabrication business, including erection workers and drawing office staff.

1983: B.& P. Lowestoft, the largest and most modern complex of its kind in Europe, with 416 employees, launched a major new range of advanced wood window designs. Managing Director: Bob Mackie. Bill Fox joined the Joinery Department in Norwich as Director and Financial Controller.

1984: The Joinery Department lost its printing, stationery and studio sections, with loss of 11 jobs.

1986: A new Managing Director, Mr. Alan Bowkett, replaced current M.D. Bob Mackie, and a new Chairman, Mr. John Allan, replaced Chairman Ray Chenhall.

It became obvious that far eastern fabricators were enjoying the benefits of subsidised pricing policies and major decisions had to be made. In July, 1986 the Steel construction department closed with loss of 139 jobs. Mr. Don Berwick, Group Personnel Director, said the situation had become so serious that only the most drastic action would give them a chance of turning the business round. The section had lost £3.2 million since 1978, and they had often accepted contracts at a 'break-even' price, or even a loss, just to keep in operation.

In 1986, as well as taking into consideration the immense drop in private new house starts (only a third of those in the 1960s), it became obvious that the increased overheads of operating the Norwich site solely as a joinery production unit was uneconomic; but I am told it was the cost of transporting products over the appalling Norfolk road system that ultimately forced the closure of the joinery manufacturing lines in Norwich. The *Eastern Evening News* reported on 6th November 1986:'Boulton & Paul yesterday axed its last 240 manufacturing jobs in Norwich, ending a 150 year era in the city. Plans to close the joinery in March come only three months after the steel works on the Riverside site was closed, with the loss of 139 jobs. Joinery work is to be switched to Maldon or Melton Mowbray.'

On 21st DECEMBER, 1987 a new Managing Director, Mr. David Chenery replaced Mr. Alan Bowkett.

Boulton & Paul still has many employees in other parts of the country and are currently in the middle of a massive £10m. investment programme on their other three sites. The Head Office of the company, which is the largest joinery manufacturer in Europe and the market leader in the supply of wood windows to the UK building industry (producing some 20,000 windows every week), will continue to be in Norwich. They are also the fourth largest supplier of kitchens to the private new build market sector in this country, and a leading supplier of internal and external doors and stairs. Last year they returned record profits, return on capital employed showed a 25% improvement, and turnover was at record levels. They were, in fact, the most successful company within BET.

But this great Company's manufacturing days in the city are over. The many riverside buildings that once housed aircraft, flying boats, airship sections, and buildings that were erected in all parts of the world, are still and empty – only the memories and reminiscences of the men and women who worked there, many of them for most of their working lives, remind us of those memorable days. We hear of proposed grandiose schemes for this 16 acre site – I wonder if William Moore, John Hilling Barnard, William Staples Boulton and John Dawson Paul would approve?

Wrought iron sign for Riverside Works.

A. J. CALEY LIMITED

Caleys, the great confectioners, in fact began by making something entirely different. A. J. Caley came to Norwich in 1857 and established a chemist's business in London Street. In 1863, he started making mineral waters in a small cellar at the back of his shop. The business expanded rapidly, and a year later he moved to Bedford Street. Even then the larger premises were not sufficient for the ever increasing trade. His son, Edward J. Caley joined the business in 1878, and in 1880 they took over a building in Chapel Field formerly occupied by George Allen, a glove cloth weaver.

Among the aerated and other waters made were soda, potash, seltzer, lemonade, ginger ale, and of tonic beverages, quinine and iron water, chalybeate water, amara (an effervescent bitter beverage), inadore and mineral water. A speciality was ginger beer, which was brewed secundem artem. All the effervescent waters were aerated in silver-lined cylinders, thus avoiding any danger of contamination from copper salts.

The sales of soft drinks were seasonal but Mr. Caley did not like 'laying off' his workers in the winter. He looked around for something else they could do and as a consequence, in 1883, he started manufacturing cocoa. That, in turn, led to the making of chocolate in 1886.

A.J.Caley retired in 1894 and died a year later, when Frederick W. Caley joined the business. Three years later, in order to give additional work to the girls employed on preparing the frills for the chocolate boxes, they started making crackers.

In 1890 a large new factory was erected and it became a joint-stock company. By this time their mineral waters were famous, used by Royalty and Members of the House of Commons. Water was drawn from two Artesian wells 400 feet and 500 feet deep respectively. By 1904 they were employing 700 people and their chocolates and crackers were being shipped to the most remote quarters of the world. They had agencies in Canada, South Africa, Australia and India, and there was a large demand for Caleys' crackers in Paris.

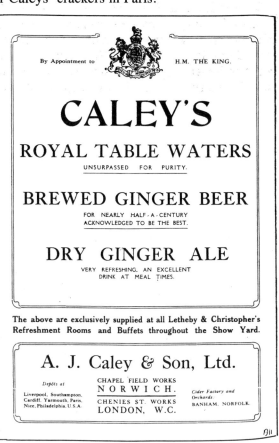

By Appointment to   H.M. THE KING.

CALEY'S

ROYAL TABLE WATERS
UNSURPASSED FOR PURITY.

BREWED GINGER BEER
FOR NEARLY HALF-A-CENTURY
ACKNOWLEDGED TO BE THE BEST.

DRY GINGER ALE
VERY REFRESHING. AN EXCELLENT
DRINK AT MEAL TIMES.

The above are exclusively supplied at all Letheby & Christopher's Refreshment Rooms and Buffets throughout the Show Yard.

A. J. Caley & Son, Ltd.

Depôts at
Liverpool, Southampton,
Cardiff, Yarmouth, Paris,
Nice, Philadelphia, U.S.A.

CHAPEL FIELD WORKS
NORWICH.
CHENIES ST. WORKS
LONDON, W.C.

Cider Factory and Orchards
BANHAM. NORFOLK.

A. J. CALEY LIMITED

The mineral water department was painstakingly described in 1904: *'Here are large gasometers for storing the carbonic acid which has been prepared with greatest care. This gas has to be incorporated with the, at present, un-aerated soda or seltzer water – as the case may be. Here is a powerful machine which, in one movement, draws gas from the gasometers and un-aerated water from large slate tanks; both are forced together into strong metal cylinders, heavily plated inside with silver. The pressure in a cylinder varies generally from 100 to 200 lbs. per square inch. From these cylinders water, now highly charged with carbolic acid gas, travels to the various machines for bottling or filling syphons. The thorough cleansing of the bottles is an important condition to successful mineral water manufacturing. The preparatory stage is soaking in hot water, after which each bottle is passed over brushes revolving at the rate of hundreds of revolutions per minute. The rinsing is done with jets of water under great pressure.*

Brewed ginger beer, for which Caleys are justly celebrated, was first brought to perfection under their aegis. Caley's brewery, which is in many respects a replica of an ordinary modern brewery, is built in tower form, in order to utilise the advantages of gravity as a means of clarifying. Huge vats and tanks are on every floor, and the place is kept spotlessly clean. In the basement is the storage cellar, which will hold 150,000 filled bottles at one time.'

At the beginning of this century a large quantity of milk chocolate was being imported from Switzerland, a chocolate vastly superior to the domestic product. Caleys decided to obtain milk of equal quality and make it on the same lines. They therefore installed a plant similar to that in Switzerland and made arrangements with a Mr. Garrett Taylor to supply them with the very best and richest milk from his celebrated Whitlingham herd of red poll cattle. This had the desired effect and Caleys were soon widely known for the quality of their milk chocolate.

Norwich made chocolate bars were popular with British troops during the first world war. Thousands of bars of Caley's famous Marching Chocolate were sent to the front, starting their journey in the firm's own solid tyred vans.

The firm remained in the hands of the Caley family until 1918, when it was purchased by The African and Eastern Trade Corporation, who in 1932, sold the firm to John Mackintosh & Sons Limited of Halifax for £138,000. The firm continued under the Chairmanship of the First Viscount Mackintosh, who was well known for his leadership of the National Savings Movement. The first pack of 'Rolo' was manufactured in Norwich in 1937, and since then its popularity has spread around the world. Today 'Rolo' is exported to over 100 countries stretching from Canada to the Cape Verde Islands, Fiji to Finland and Nepal to Nicaragua. The main 'Rolo' plant at Norwich produces two tons in one hour.

Early delivery vans

Photo: Rowntree Mackintosh

World War Two brought a substantial setback when in 1942 an incendiary raid on Norwich caused a fire which spread rapidly and totally destroyed the works. The rebuilding of the factory on the old site started in 1946, allowing limited production facilities to operate, and the first phase of the reconstruction was completed in 1949. The whole rebuilding scheme was not completed until 1952. In 1956 H.R.H. The Duchess of Kent opened the completed Norwich factory and offices. There followed a succession of new products. Week-End and Munchies were introduced in 1957, and Caramac was started in 1959. Good News Assortment began in production at Norwich in 1960.

Meanwhile, the mineral water business was sold to a local brewery after the war and the manufacture of Christmas crackers was carried on by an associated company, Caleys Crackers Limited, with premises in Salhouse Road; now Tom Smith & Company Limited.

The first two stages of a roof-top car park for employees were completed in 1963, with room for 157 cars, and the final two stages in 1967 provided an additional 110 spaces. This was the first of such schemes in the city. The Harold Mackintosh memorial flats for pensioners were opened in 1968.

Following the integration of the Mackintosh and Rowntree operations in 1969, the Norwich factory has played an important role in the continued development of the Rowntree Mackintosh business,

both in the U.K. and around the world. The Rowntree Mackintosh group has received the Queen's Award for Exports on three separate occasions. Today on the Chapel Field site, which covers approximately seven acres, water from the same artesian wells is used in the chocolate making process, but almost nothing in the factory is now wrapped or made by hand. Only in centre making and packing are traditional methods used. Modern plants like 'Yorkie' use only a quarter of the labour of the older plants, and produce a greater output per hour. A computer controlled ingredient system has been installed, replacing manual labour and leading to more consistent use of materials.

Today the Company employs about 1,100 people in Norwich and 17,000 throughout the Group in the United Kingdom. The Norwich factory manufactures over 40 million chocolate eggs each year in preparation for Easter.

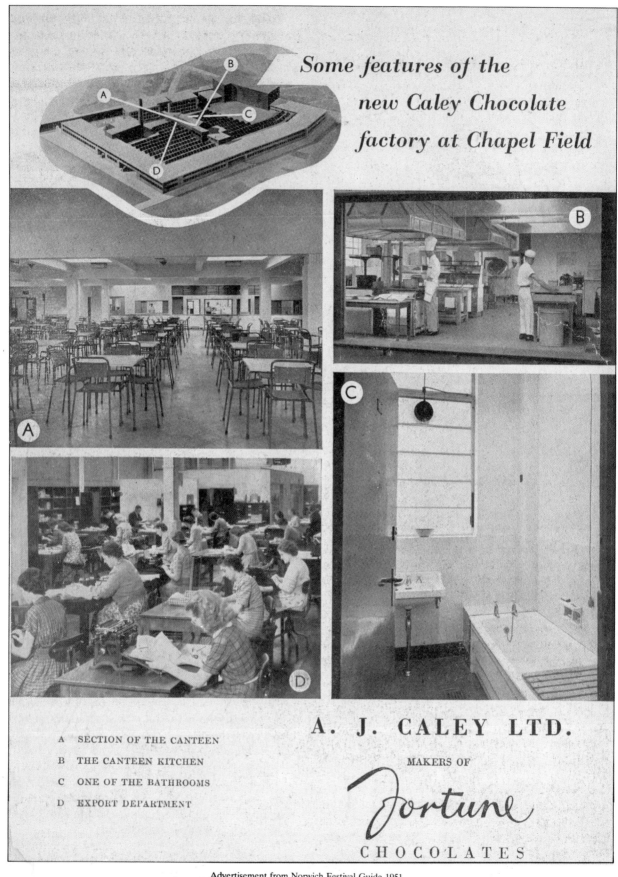

Some features of the new Caley Chocolate factory at Chapel Field

A   SECTION OF THE CANTEEN
B   THE CANTEEN KITCHEN
C   ONE OF THE BATHROOMS
D   EXPORT DEPARTMENT

A. J. CALEY LTD.

MAKERS OF

Fortune

CHOCOLATES

Advertisement from Norwich Festival Guide 1951.

BARNARDS LIMITED

On 9th November 1826 Charles Barnard (1804-1871) started up in business as an Ironmonger, Oil and Colourman, in premises near Norwich Market. By 1840 he had added to the retail business workshops in Pottergate for the manufacture of ironwork for domestic and agricultural implements.

He was the son of a farmer and knew there was a need for fencing to keep out rabbits and foxes. It is said he started to experiment with cotton reels, and when he had established the practicability of the idea, pegged rollers were made for the production of black japanned netting. These rollers were supported on iron trestles and the fabric was woven by men who were provided with bobbins carrying the gauge of wire required. The size of the mesh depended on the peg spacings. Production was slow and Mr. Barnard decided to try and design a machine. He succeeded, and by 1844 a primitive loom, using a man as a weaver, with a boy to power the machine, was being used in his works. He used the 'Half Wheel' principle by which two slides and a rack engaged alternately to form the twists. This invention, although not patented, must place Barnard high on the list of innovative inventors of his time. The original machine is in working order and can still be seen at the Bridewell Museum in Norwich.

Cast iron frame lighthouse built by Barnard Bishop & Barnards off the coast of Brazil, 1860.

Chicken House by Barnard Bishop & Barnards.

Norfolk Museums Service

In 1846 John Bishop, from St. Ives, became a partner, and the rapidly increasing business then necessitated the removal of the works to larger premises in St. George's, Colegate, and Calvert Street. In 1859 Charles' two eldest sons became partners and the firm became Barnard, Bishop & Barnard. In the 1861 census Charles Barnard was listed as proprietor of the works where 105 workmen were employed, with 47 lads, 7 clerks and 4 shopmen.

The ever expanding business led to another move, this time to St. Michael's, Coslany. They erected new buildings to house the Netting Mill and steam power was used to power the looms. They called the factory The Norfolk Iron Works and made a wide variety of goods, including very ornate fireplaces.

A.D. Bayne writing in 1869, described the new works: *'The important works of Barnard, Bishop & Barnard, are situate in St. Michael's, Coslany, and cover an area of one acre, next the River Wensum. Entering from Coslany Street, the new Counting House is joined on the right by a suite of offices, and on the left by the smith's shop, which is backed by fire-proof workshops, seventy-five feet in length, and five stories in height. The large foundry is at the east end of the works. A tramway runs from Coslany Street into the interior, permeating the premises. About 400 men and boys are engaged.'*

Thomas Jekyll was a fireplace designer, and he introduced oriental effects into Barnards' products. He was an architect, who lived in The Close, and was a close friend of Sands, the artist, who painted a portrait of George Barnard.

Jekyll designed the 'Norwich Gates', pillars and railings. They were exhibited in London and awarded a medal for design and art work. These gates were only 13 feet wide and 7 feet in height but occupied 40 of the best workmen from morning till night for three months at a cost of £750 in wages. There was not a touch of the chisel, the hammer did all the work in the most perfect manner. They were bought by the residents of Norfolk and Norwich and given to the Prince of Wales in 1864 as a wedding present. They now form the entrance to The Royal Park at Sandringham.

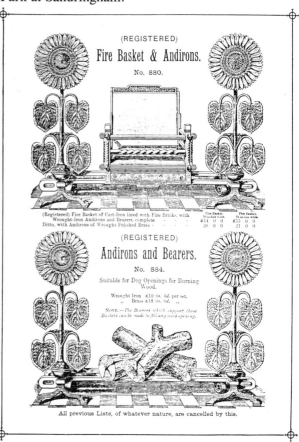

Charles Barnard died in 1871 and was buried in Booton churchyard. By the following year the firm were designing and installing central heating

U M B R E L L A   C A N O P Y.

The above engraving represents an Umbrella Canopy, 6 feet in diameter, the price of which is   1 10 0
If with Fly Curtains to protect from wind 2 2 0
If with Walls all round to form a tent   .   2 10 0

Full particulars of Chairs, Tables, &c., as shown above, will be found at Pages 51, 61, 71, and 75.

All previous Lists, of whatever nature, are cancelled by this.

systems for Norwich Cathedral and St. Peter Mancroft church.

Another conspicuous structure was a Pagoda built of wrought and cast iron, which was exhibited at the 1876 Philadelphia Exhibition, and awarded a Prize Medal. It was also shown at the 1878 Paris Exhibition. Purchased by Norwich Corporation for £500, it was erected in Chapel Field Gardens. It stayed there until after the Second World War, but was considered too rusty and unsafe for people to use and was eventually demolished. Some of the attractive ornamental sun-flowers which decorated the Pagoda can still be seen in Heigham Park, near the tennis courts.

Other notable projects were:-

1880 A Railway bridge built over the River Wensum between Norwich and Lenwade.

1881 The Roof of the Agricultural Hall.

1882 City Station bridge, which crossed the Wensum from Barn Road to St. Martin's Street (now Oak Street) (If you can escape the rush of traffic on what is now the inner link road, take a look at the bridge – the makers' name is there for all to see).

1886 Ornamental roof, gates and railings for City Station. Thorpe Station barrier which was designed by W. Neville Ashbee, ARIBA.

In 1887 Barnards became a Limited Company and Mr. James Bower took an active part in the affairs of

the firm. By the beginning of the 20th century he had re-designed and re-built all the wire netting machinery and invented a special machine for weaving mixed mesh wire netting which was patented. Many thousands of miles of this netting were supplied to Australia for rabbit fencing.

The company became known as Barnards Limited in 1907 with Mr. Bower as Managing Director.

Pavilion in Chapelfield Gardens

During the 1914/18 War Barnards supplied the Government with upwards of 7,000 miles of wire netting for road making across the Egyptian desert and the formation of revetments to trenches in the War Zone.

The desire for innovation was ever-present. As the difficulty in procuring spelter for the galvanizing process increased, the idea of coating the netting with tar varnish was suggested, and the Company immediately put down extensive plant comprising dipping tanks and drying ovens to deal with it; thereafter this finish was exclusively adopted by the departments concerned.

In addition to the netting, the Company produced many hundreds of yards of special hand-woven wire lattice for the Balkan theatre of war; large heating stoves for the American army in France; wire screens for high explosive factories; hundreds of tons of castings for the Admiralty and other departments; and cooking ranges and heating stoves for the various camps and training centres. Two hundred of the workers enlisted, and fifteen died, including the Managing Director's son, Mr. Charles F. Bower, who was killed near Hill 60, just as he had been gazetted to the rank of Captain.

In 1921 part of the old Mousehold Aerodrome was purchased for a storage site. Between the wars they continued to make a great variety of items, and in 1928 started manufacturing chain link fencing, which was considerably stronger than the wire netting.

After the outbreak of the Second World War Barnards turned to the manufacture of gun shells at their factory on Mousehold. They employed 1,200 people who worked on the production of 4.5 inch gun shells, 4.5 inch howitzers, anti-tank mortar

Station platform and canopy made by Barnards for the new Thorpe Station opened in 1886.

bombs, and parts for the Hurricane aircraft. Three quarters of a million telegraph poles were made for the North Africa campaign, as well as ammunition trucks, and wire netting for temporary airfield runways. They also produced propellers and stern gear assemblies for motor torpedo boats for the Japanese War.

On Tuesday, 9th July, 1940, at 5 p.m. two aircraft were seen approaching the factory from the north-east. No alert had been sounded, but when the employees saw the ominous black crosses on the wings they ran to take shelter. The raid only lasted six seconds – two people died and others suffered minor injuries. The hangars and other buildings on the site were hit by twelve high explosive bombs. My father, who was there at the time, came home that night with huge pieces of shrapnel that had landed close to where he and many others had flung themselves to the ground.

Another air-raid took place on 27th February, 1941, but there were no casualties although further damage was caused to the buildings. Happily the company managed to continue with its war effort despite these raids.

In 1955 Barnards became part of Tinsley Wire Industries of Sheffield, and since then they have concentrated on the production of Wire Fencing Products at the 15 acre site on Salhouse Road. Chain link fencing was made in plastic and galvanized

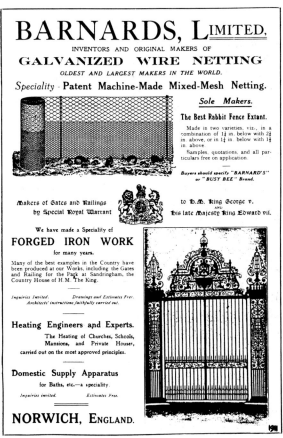

Advetisement from 1911 showing the Sandringham Gates.

BARNARDS LIMITED

coated wire and in 1960 they started manufacturing Norfence, an ornamental fencing for use in gardens.

Tinsley took over Boulton & Paul's wire products division in 1964 and it was merged with Barnards, and in 1976 they celebrated 150 years of trading. In 1979 Tinsley purchased Flexipane Limited and this was incorporated into the production at the Mousehold Works.

The 'Oil Boom' meant Barnards were again looking for new ideas. They invented a kind of netting to lag and reinforce the concrete around the oil pipes which go under the sea. They were making about 100 miles per day to meet the export demands from the Far East.

Today this firm, which grew from a small ironmonger's shop at the back of Norwich Market Place, is known all over the world, and although it does not make the variety of goods it once did, still prides itself on the excellence and quality of the products and is the leading manufacturer of wire fencing in the United Kingdom.

Conclusion

I am sure all Norwich people are interested in the way their city is developing. In the 18th century labouring people left the Norfolk countryside to work in Norwich, lured by the prospect of jobs and higher wages. They lived in the tiny houses which had infilled many of the previous open spaces, gardens and yards. Many families of ten or more persons were crammed into two-roomed houses, sharing one privy in the yard with many others, and a water pump that only operated at certain times of the day. They worked long hours for very little pay, and hunger and disease were never far away. The more prosperous members of the Norwich community were, however, moving out to large houses in the suburbs and surrounding countryside.

Colmans, the great manufacturers of mustard, moved from Stoke Mill to Norwich in 1857, and provided jobs, a canteen, and 'after hours' activities for their workers. Several large engineering companies had their factories in the city, the drink trade flourished and four large breweries provided liquid refreshment for Norfolk throats. Printing works were established, and many small firms connected with the major industries made their home in Norwich. Specialist shops were opened to cater for the increase in local and County trade, and the coming of the railway in 1844 helped to increase the volume of Norwich goods sent all over the country, and overseas.

In the early part of this century trade and industry had taken over the city. Iron foundries belched out smoke and the factories provided work for thousands of people. By mid-century the pattern had altered. The City Council provided housing estates in the suburbs for the workers, and the availability of public transport made living outside the city walls easier for everyone.

Today it is interesting to see how the city is once again changing. The 1975 Heritage Scheme brought good new housing back to the centre, and this trend has continued with the Anchor Brewery site, and other projects in King Street, Quayside and Rouen Road. Industry has, with very few exceptions, moved out to the many industrial estates on the outskirts. The Castle Mall Scheme, now agreed between the Council and the developers, will bring additional modern shopping and hotel facilities into the city centre.

It is probably a good thing to entice people back to live in the city, and to build large superstores and offices, but I do hope that some of the old established shops and businesses, names that I have known from childhood, will survive. Window shopping in Norwich has always been an enjoyable experience – I doubt if its citizens get as much pleasure looking at the present displays of the many Estate Agents and Building Societies!

Bibliography

Banger, J., Norwich At War (1974)

Barfield, T.J., Scott Built a Dynamo (1968)

Barringer, J.C., (Ed.) Norwich in the Nineteenth Century (1984)

Bayne, A.D., A Brief History of Norwich and its Manufactures (1864)

Bignold, Sir Robert, Five Generations of the Bignold Family (1948)

Bullard, H.H., Sir Harry Bullard, M.P. (1902)

Burgess, E. & W.L., Men Who Made Norwich (1904)

Citizens of No Mean City (1910)

Copeman, W.O., Copemans of Norwich 1789-1946 (1946)

Copeman, W.O., Copemans of Norwich 1789-1964 (1965)

Downing, J., Copemans of Norwich 1789-1973 (Norfolk Fair) (1973)

Goose, H.H., Norwich Under Water 1878 and 1912 (1912)

Gourvish, Terry, Norfolk Beers from English Barley (1987)

Harry Bullard, Esq. (1882)

Hawkins, C.B., Norwich: A Social Study (1910)

Illustrated Record of the Great Flood (1912)

Jarrold's Norwich Trade Directories (Various)

John Mackintosh & Sons Ltd, The Mackintosh Story (1967)

Kelly's Norfolk & Norwich Directories (Various)

Leaf and The Tree. The (Boulton & Paul) (1947)

Leeds, H., (Ed.) Peace souvenir – Norwich War Record (1920)

Munnings, Sir A., An Artist's Life (1950)

Norwich and Its region. British Association for the Advancement of Science (1961)

Palgrave-Moore, P., Mayors and Lord Mayors of Norwich 1836-1974 (1978)

Read, Ltd., R.J. The History of the Firm 1875-1949 (1949)

Retrospect. A., Barnards Ltd 1844-1911 (1911)

Social Register of the County of Norfolk (1935)

Sparks, W.L., Shoemaking in Norwich (1949)

Townroe, Peter M., Norwich: A Time of Opportunity (1988)

Who's Who in Norwich (1961)